THE REST

OF

THE STORY

THE REST

OF

THE STORY

Arthur Laurents

A LIFE COMPLETED

APPLAUSE
THEATRE & CINEMA BOOKS
Guilford, Connecticut

APPLAUSE
THEATRE & CINEMA BOOKS

An imprint of Globe Pequot, the trade division of
The Rowman & Littlefield Publishing Group, Inc.
4501 Forbes Blvd., Ste. 200
Lanham, MD 20706
www.rowman.com

Distributed by NATIONAL BOOK NETWORK

Published in 2012 by Applause Theatre & Cinema Books
An Imprint of Hal Leonard Corporation
7777 West Bluemound Road
Milwaukee, WI 53213

Trade Book Division Editorial Offices
33 Plymouth St., Montclair, NJ 07042

Grateful acknowledgment is made to W. W. Norton & Company, Inc. for permission to reprint
"The Layers." Copyright © 1978 by Stanley Kunitz, from *The Collected Poems* by Stanley Kunitz.
Used by permission of W. W. Norton & Company, Inc.

Grateful acknowledgement is made to Stephen Sondheim for permission to reprint
"The Arthur Laurents Birthday Song" lyrics.

All photographs are from the author's collection.

Book design by Michael Kellner

British Library Cataloguing in Publication Information available

Library of Congress Cataloging-in-Publication Data
Names: Laurents, Arthur, author.
Title: The rest of the story : a life completed / Arthur Laurents.
Description: Guilford, Connecticut : Applause Books, [2022] | Includes bibliographical references
 and index. | Summary: "Laurents passed away early in 2011, but not before writing The Rest of
 the Story, in which he revealed all that had happened in his life since Original Story By, filled with
 the wisdom he gained in growing older and a new perspective brought on by Laurents' experience
 of deep personal loss, including the death of his longtime companion, Tom Hatcher"— Provided
 by publisher.
Identifiers: LCCN 2021053613 (print) | LCCN 2021053614 (ebook) | ISBN9781493065226
 (paperback) | ISBN 9781480302426 (ebook)
Subjects: LCSH: Laurents, Arthur. | Dramatists, American—20thcentury—Biography. | Motion
 picture producers and directors—UnitedStates—Biography. | Theatrical producers and
 directors—UnitedStates—Biography. | Screenwriters—United States—Biography.
Classification: LCC PS3523.A827 Z46 2022 (print) | LCC PS3523.A827 (ebook) | DDC 812/.52
 [B]—dc23/eng/20211101
LC record available at https://lccn.loc.gov/2021053613
LC ebook record available at https://lccn.loc.gov/2021053614

CONTENTS

FOREWORD

———

by Bernadette Peters

I met Arthur when we both had a professional disappointment of sorts. He was happy to tell me there was light at the end of the tunnel, because he now was there. He was a bit ahead of me on that one. He said he was writing and having his plays produced and feeling better than ever. That was encouraging and very sweet and generous of him. We shared that experience.

Many years later, we shared another experience—we shared loss. He lost his partner of fifty-two years, Tom Hatcher. In that instance, I was there to help him. I was ahead of him on this one, losing my husband the year before in a helicopter accident.

A month or so later, I got a phone call. Arthur was thinking of directing *Gypsy*, and I encouraged him to do it. After his loss, I knew he needed something to occupy his time, and that it would be important to him.

I cherished the close relationship we had toward the end of his life. Of course, I didn't know it was the end of his life. As Arthur expresses in this book, he was planning to live to one hundred, and he was in amazing shape. He went skiing that year and had a young and exuberant attitude. He just seemed ongoing.

It was very touching to read this book, as I realized it was a tribute to the love of his life, Tom. Interestingly, I don't think Arthur realized just how important Tom was to him till he started going over his life. Arthur, during the last three years of his life, came to the realization that love, above all else, above writing, directing, the theater—Tom's love—was the most important thing that had happened to him.

As Arthur wrote about Tom, "Just being there gave me a sense of security, a calmness, a feeling that all was well and always would be. Nothing and no one can replace that." He added, "Just the memory helps though."

INTRODUCTION

by David Saint

One year before his death on May 5, 2011, Arthur Laurents decided to reread his controversial memoir, *Original Story By*. The piece had been published over a decade earlier.

On finishing, he turned to me and said, "I have to write the rest of the story. The world has changed since then, the theatre has changed, and I've changed."

He finished this new book, his last work, exactly one week before he died.

Certainly the world as he knew it had changed, both literally and figuratively, after 9/11. Arthur's longtime residence in Greenwich Village looked straight down Seventh Avenue at those two billowing clouds of smoke that covered even the steps of his beautiful brownstone. He was in the process of writing a new play about an American filmmaker and a beautiful Turkish woman, called *Attacks on the Heart*. I remember him calling me after putting aside the script, saying, "I can't do it anymore. I can't write. Nothing is the same."

It was the first time I had ever heard Arthur say he could no longer write. I would hear him say that twice more.

The Beginning of the Story: *Arthur, the writer, at home.*

But about a month later he decided to return to his computer and, in typical Arthur fashion, incorporate the cataclysmic event of that day into his story, now challenging the very essence of patriotism and questioning the effect of xenophobia on his world and on his play.

Throughout the following years, he felt the theatre had changed, and therefore decided to revisit his two great masterpieces of musical theatre, *Gypsy* and *West Side Story*. In each case, he had found a reason to look at the piece with a new point of view, one that reflected his own changing approach to the process of directing. He was now much more interested in exploring the deeper character motivations behind those iconic roles of Rose, Herbie, Louise, Tony, Maria, Anita, and the others.

The next cataclysmic event in his life, and the second time he decided to stop writing, was on October 26, 2006. The day Tom Hatcher died.

This time he said, "He was my reason for living. My reason for writing." It would be months before he could turn back to the keyboard again. That time it would be to write a heartbreaking story of loss called *Come Back, Come Back, Wherever You Are*.

Ironically, Arthur had written his most blatantly autobiographical play to date, *Two Lives*, a few years earlier, long before Tom grew ill, in which the "Tom" character clutches his chest and utters, "What's this?" falls over and dies at the end of Act One. I remember reading that scene sitting on the bench in their beloved park in Quogue and dropping the script on the grass, yelling to Arthur, "You can't kill Tom!" Act Two went on to explore the "Arthur" character's desperate attempt to carry on living.

I will never forget the opening night at George Street, when Tom

KELLY RYMAN

The Bench: *The secret garden that is home.*

stood shaken and alone on the sidewalk in front of the theatre. I asked him if he was okay. He turned to me, pale as a ghost, and said, "He's written me dead."

When I read aloud a scene from *Two Lives* at Tom's memorial in the park, Arthur turned to me, still in a daze, and said, "How did I know that?"

You see, at the time, Arthur felt he was writing two fictional characters, even if the world saw Arthur and Tom. But Arthur always wrote about the many sides of himself and his life and never saw it as anything but characters in a fiction.

One time he mentioned to me that some well-known journalist had asked him, "Where did Rose come from? Was your mother like that?" He'd responded, "No, nothing like that." By that time I knew Arthur better than anyone. I looked him straight in the eye and said, "I know where Rose came from. She's you."

He stared right back at me and after a long pause said simply, "You're a witch."

Arthur continued to write new plays right up until his death. But this last memoir needed to be finished. The notion of change, even as he wrote each new chapter, fascinated him. In fact, the process of writing this book included returning to each chapter nearly a year later and updating each "change" with an even newer perspective. I read a poem at that time, called "The Layers," by poet laureate Stanley Kunitz, who had recently passed away at 100. I gave it to Arthur and he was deeply affected by it. "That's it," he said. "That's what I'm feeling."

"Change" was the theme, the prism through which this last memoir was to be viewed. As you read, you may notice that certain stories or scenes have been told in fragments in other books of his, most notably *Original Story By*. However, the point is that, in *Rashomon*-like fashion, they are seen now from a different perspective, the byproduct of "change."

The third and last time I heard Arthur say he could no longer write was sitting together in a waiting room at Mt. Sinai a few days before his death.

I was trying to encourage him to fight this pneumonia, and he said, "David . . . my hands are shaking so badly I can't use the computer, my vision is blurry, I can't write anymore. If I can't write, I can't live."

I knew then he had finished the rest of the story.

The story was over and so was he.

The Layers

by Stanley Kunitz

———

I have walked through many lives,
some of them my own,
and I am not who I was,
though some principle of being
abides, from which I struggle
not to stray.
When I look behind,
as I am compelled to look
before I can gather strength
to proceed on my journey,
I see the milestones dwindling
toward the horizon
and the slow fires trailing
from the abandoned camp-sites,
over which scavenger angels
wheel on heavy wings.
Oh, I have made myself a tribe
out of my true affections,
and my tribe is scattered!
How shall the heart be reconciled
to its feast of losses?
In a rising wind
the manic dust of my friends,
those who fell along the way,
bitterly stings my face.

Yet I turn, I turn,
exulting somewhat,
with my will intact to go
wherever I need to go,
and every stone on the road
precious to me.
In my darkest night,
when the moon was covered
and I roamed through wreckage,
a nimbus-clouded voice
directed me:
"Live in the layers,
not on the litter."
Though I lack the art
to decipher it,
no doubt the next chapter
in my book of transformations
is already written.
I am not done with my changes.

ONE

Change

Change is what keeps us alive to life. It's given me a new perspective on everything from the nature of friendship to the writing of a play. I'm ninety-three and still changing. I've learned (yet again) not to expect as much from a treasured friend, but I have also just finished a play unlike any I have ever written.

In the decade between the publication of my memoir *Original Story By* and now, I have changed constantly. The man I was in 2000 is, in some respects, the same, but in others, many others, he is quite different. I've learned what I wasn't even aware had to be learned: that just because something is true, you don't have to write it. Nor do you have to say it, although I still have to stop myself from doing that.

In that memoir, I wrote a good deal about sex. I held sex to be one of the most important things in life, second only to love. I wouldn't put it second today; today, love is first, it always will be; then comes friendship; then come writing and the theatre; and *then* comes sex. That ranking isn't because I'm ninety-three and retired sexually. I'm ninety-three and unretired.

No matter where I rank it now or then, in *Original Story By,* I wrote about my sex life too much, too often, and included too many names, especially Farley Granger. There I am, telling truths I felt should be told. Truths do not demand to be told. Farley did not ask to be exposed. I was unfair and unkind to someone I loved. I should not have written what I did and I apologize in writing. It's late but not too late; Farley and I are on good terms today. We've both changed.

Today, I would red-pencil much of what I wrote about my sexual life in that memoir. It would hurt sales—there is still the occasional buyer. Many famous theatre and movie names are dropped in that book—its subtitle is *A Memoir of Broadway and Hollywood*—but when its readers speak about it to me, as they do to this day (and isn't that nice), it isn't those names they talk about. It's one thing—I was about to say "one thing by and large," but with this subject, unwanted double meanings abound. Simply, then, the one thing they mainly talk about is my sexual cavorting. Well, I'm in my nineties, fairly well preserved, very much alive, and so they speculate. Often their comments are tinged with admiration, sometimes envy, but with the young—commonality. They take it for granted I will understand the cavorting they're talking about and will be in favor. They're right.

Here, I must interrupt myself because it's August 24, the day that heralded the biggest change in my life. The twenty-fourth is Tom Hatcher's birthday, the day we met and our anniversary, because a few days later we fell in love and began fifty-two years of sharing every aspect of our lives. Those years gave me an unimaginably happy life for which I'm still grateful and always will be.

When we met in Hollywood, he was twenty-five and from Tulsa,

The Golden Boy: *Tom at twenty-five.*

Oklahoma; I was thirty-seven and from New York, New York—but he was far wiser and more knowing. Everyone thought I called the shots, but he did, and I liked it. I loved him, he loved me, we didn't ask for anything more. During the years, he changed, I changed, there were less than desirable periods, but we always knew the love was there and we would always be together. Life was so good, we took too much for granted. It didn't occur to us it might end the way it did. In the turn of the century year 2000, I wrote at the end of *Original Story By*:

   From Tom's pool, you can see into the heart of the park.

This is a beautiful private park in Quogue that he created out of a dark jungle of trees strangled by bittersweet vines. He divided it into what he called "rooms." On the northern perimeter, he built a big house with a pool for us. The beach house was small. Not so small today, when there is only me.

Refuge: *The pool (and park beyond) in Quogue.*

KELLY RYMAN

Writer's Perch: *The bench where Arthur read each work aloud to Tom.*

In summer, we do laps every day. Often, we walk through the park, then sit on that bench, looking at the view.

This is something I just did. I do it whenever I want to be with him.

Yesterday, we sat there a little longer than usual, just looking at the changing light, not saying anything. But Tom reads my mind.

"You're going to live twenty more years," he assured me. Maybe even more. As long as he lives, I will.

* * *

But on October 26, 2006, Tom died of lung cancer. The loss brought the most devastating change in my life and almost destroyed me. When, months later, I could again see there was a world and people in it, I had changed as never before. Friendship had an importance it had never had. Loss does that. I had love to give; I gave it to a few friends. They were waiting, they requited the love. The meaning of friendship changed.

Since then, I have changed several times, seeing people and events differently each time. Only a few weeks ago, just after my ninety-third birthday, my eyes ceased welling up at the mention, even the thought of the name "Tom." The pain was gone. It took three and a half years plus, but the loss is bearable and invisible now. A welcome change.

In the Letters to the Times this morning, there was a debate among psychiatrists backed up by quotes from a psychiatric manual about the amount of time allowed for grieving over a death. Some thought it should be two weeks, some thought it should be two months before the griever was judged to be in a major depression and should be medicated.

I was helped to survive Tom's death by others who had been in my situation a year or two or more. The youngest was fifty-one. All of us were grieving over the loss of a person we had been in love with. The people I have been trying to help—the youngest is in his eighties— have also lost a person he or she was in love with. Perhaps these psychiatrists and their clients are of a much younger generation, and the clients were suffering the loss of someone they were in like with. Or perhaps the psychiatrists were dealing with veterinaries.

When Tom came to live with me in New York—this was 1955— we lived openly without thinking that it wasn't what was done if you had any public identity, even what little I had. Being gay was never a problem for him. He said the moment he knew he was gay he knew he had to leave Oklahoma. He never had the problems others did. Well, he was extraordinary, as everyone who knew him knew. What shouldn't have been surprising to me was that it took his death to make me aware of that, or that everyone who met him wanted him to like them. My love for him was so dominating I felt he wasn't appreciated. Consequently, I kept talking about him and writing about him. And now? Now I write about him because I'm writing about change and Tom is the reason for the two biggest changes in my life and in me—love and death.

At the end of the sixties, when Judy Garland's funeral and the Stonewall riots begat gay liberation, Tom and I lived in a place where it wasn't needed—the West Village, on one of the prettiest streets in the city. Couples liked to stroll down that street, St. Luke's Place. On one side, gingko trees shelter a row of Italianate brownstones built in 1852; on the other side, a public library, an outdoor swimming pool, and a playground. The strollers were of all genders and colors, but nobody noticed, not on that street or any street in the Village. All that changed in the eighties with the arrival of AIDS. The Village was decimated; we lost friends. And the country turned out not to be so liberated after all: it hadn't changed very much. Gay retook its place at the top of the unwanted minority list and held firm through 2009, when *Brokeback Mountain* wasn't awarded the Oscar it merited and Heath Ledger wasn't awarded the Oscar he merited for his performance in that openly gay love story.

Liberation never had meaning for me until I began writing *Mainly on Directing* in 2009. I had begun writing derogatively about married gays but stopped mid-phrase—its meaning had changed. Gays had

A New York Classic: *The Greenwich Village brownstone*
that was home for over fifty years.

been getting married legally since Massachusetts recognized the right in 2004. My opinion of gay men who pretended not to be when they married a woman didn't change. Marriage for two gay men was another matter.

Tom and I had talked about it. We hadn't felt the need. But at that time, neither of us knew that there are literally over 1400 legal advantages to being married. Practical advantages like hospital visitation rights as well as mutual tax returns and other financial advantages. If Tom were alive today, we would have gotten married, no question.

I read the marriage notices in the Sunday Times. There are always one or two announcing the union of a gay or lesbian couple, sometimes even with photographs. To me, "gay" includes both genders, but I bow here to clumsy political correctness. The status level is high, but it is for all the Times couples. Status means money. How else do they get there? Nonetheless, we are there.

The country's attitude toward gay marriage has been changing constantly. The political hard right doesn't change, however; it continues to use same-sex marriage as a political football and continues to kick the hell out of it with Proposition 8.

Prop. 8 is the California ballot measure that banned same-sex marriage but was overturned by a judge who declared the measure clearly unconstitutional. As expected, the exceptionally long and well-reasoned decision went to the Ninth Circuit Court of Appeals and was expected to be appealed from there to the Supreme Court. That court, the Roberts Court, is the most right-wing in history: it decided that a corporation has the same constitutional rights as an individual citizen. What a California judge deemed clearly unconstitutional, the Roberts Court might twist and turn into clearly constitutional. However, it may never get to Roberts & Co., for the Ninth Circuit Court of Appeals is asking whether those appealing the overturn have any legal standing to appeal.

This is the type of issue I once would have been actively involved in, but I have changed. I have become inactive politically. I stay out of it because, like most of the country, in the last year of Obama, I have lost hope. Whatever he may achieve in his presidency, Barack Obama will forever be tainted for sending thousands of young American men and women to Afghanistan to be destroyed physically or mentally for a highly questionable political purpose in a war that no one can ever win. In his campaign year, he advocated getting out of Afghanistan at once. Has he changed, or was he never what we hoped he was because we needed hope? That's one thing that never changes—the need for hope. At the end of an early play of mine, *A Clearing in the Woods,* there is the line: "An end to dreams is not the end of hope." I have long given up dreams but never hope.

Original Story By tracks my political activism from the thirties, when I went to Cornell, through World War II, when I did radio propaganda and was investigated as possibly being a Communist (since I was in the Amy, if the charge had been true, I would have been thrown into Leavenworth, the Federal slammer), peaking in the forties in Hollywood with the arrival of the House Un-American Activities Committee. The Committee was ostensibly in town to root out Communism in the motion picture industry. The Committee knew there was no Communism in the movies; it also knew there were Communists in town; its purpose was to make political hay. What better helpers to make headlines then the movies and movie stars?

The Hollywood Witch Hunt, as it was known, changed Hollywood forever. I was never called to testify, but I was blacklisted, changing my life forever.

All this is in *The Way We Were,* which came directly out of my life at Cornell as well as in Hollywood. Katie Morosky, the campus

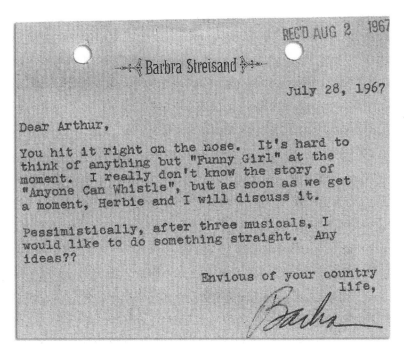

RECD AUG 2 1967

⤙ Barbra Streisand ⤚

July 28, 1967

Dear Arthur,

You hit it right on the nose. It's hard to think of anything but "Funny Girl" at the moment. I really don't know the story of "Anyone Can Whistle", butt as soon as we get a moment, Herbie and I will discuss it.

Pessimistically, after three musicals, I would like to do something straight. Any ideas??

Envious of your country life,

Barbra

The Way They Would Be: *Barbra wrote this request just months before Arthur wrote* The Way We Were *for her.*

political progressive played by Barbra Streisand, is mainly me. Undoubtedly, that accounted to a large extent for why I was so upset at the time and for long after by what the director did to the picture. Totally ignorant of the period, he destroyed its politics. And I had chosen him. I had persuaded Streisand to take him. My enthusiasm was based on his movie *They Shoot Horses, Don't They?*

I saw that picture again the other day. I was horrified to see that it wasn't good, the director was more interested in the camera than the actors, who were unbelievable because of what he had them do physically. The movie is about a dance marathon and as the days went on, the presumably exhausted contestants were running around and fighting as though they had just come out of the shower. It was made in 1969. Has my taste changed so much?

Certainly I have. Today, *The Way We Were* is a love story, period. I'm gratified it's regarded as a classic love story and people bring out the Kleenex when it's shown on television.

My play *Jolson Sings Again* is about the product of the witch hunt that haunted me the most: the informers. Elia Kazan and Jerome Robbins got the biggest headlines. I knew Jerry very well; Gadge, not as well. The line in the play—"You aren't evil because you informed, you informed because you're evil"—is me talking to Jerry. Their work was admirable, their behavior contemptible.

For years, I crusaded against informers in general, those two in particular. I was tainted because I worked with each after I knew he was an informer—tainted because to work with an informer was to validate an informer. Any explanation is only an explanation, not an excuse. Nonetheless, the crusading continued; it's even in *Original Story By*. I could not speak about Jerry or Kazan without castigating them for being informers. It matters less now, but it matters. My guess is that it always will.

Today, if I speak of them at all, it's about their work.

I have changed, obviously. But it's the change in the country that has brought a completely new perspective. Informers don't exist. Monica Lewinsky was not considered an informer; she was a sexy girl in a semen-sequined dress blabbing about unofficial business in the Oval Office. It was the President's denial that brought on the impeachment trial.

No, today there are no informers. There are leaks and leakers and blogs and bloggers, daily character destruction minute by minute on the ubiquitous Internet. An informer is merely one who gives out information.

In the late fifties, I did two shows with Jerry Robbins that changed my status in the theatre but didn't change me: *West Side Story* and *Gypsy*. Today, both are classics; back in '57 and '59 respectively, each was a success with a mixed reception.

The four creators of *West Side*—Leonard Bernstein, Jerome Robbins, Stephen Sondheim and I—had a glorious time inventing the show. When its first performance in Washington, D.C., rocked the city, Jerry became an ego-monster. My interest in the show ended. It had diminished during rehearsals because *West Side* had become all about the dancing. The music was magnificent but it was poorly sung and the acting of anything was non-existent. The love story wasn't told.

The movie was a great hit, but I didn't like it for too many reasons—the gangs were color-coordinated chorus boys dancing down real streets, the skin of the Puerto Ricans was darkened by Max Factor and their accents were insulting to real Puerto Ricans, etc. It's also probably the worst-acted musical ever filmed. *West Side Story* meant nothing to me until Tom went to Bogotá in 2005.

He always had to have a project in addition to taking care of all his properties in Quogue, all our business, and all of me. Creating his park in summer was a project, but there was the rest of the year. So he studied Spanish, became fluent in the language, and began visiting at least the capital of every country in South America. Sometimes, I went with him. I even went to Bogotá with him but wasn't with him when he saw *West Side Story* there in Spanish. Since the Sharks were speaking the hometown language, that made them the heroes and the Jets the villains. Tom's reaction was the source of the Sharks speaking and singing in Spanish in the show. The concept intrigued me so much I wanted, for the first time, to direct *West Side Story*.

Rebirth: *The Bogotá production that prompted Tom to suggest a bilingual reimagining of* West Side Story.

At the same time, Tom urged me to direct a production of *Gypsy*, starring Patti LuPone, at New York's City Center. He felt strongly that the memory of the last Broadway production had to be supplanted by a new *Gypsy* that was what *Gypsy* should be.

I took on both because of my love for him. And then he died. As I said, that changed me. He used to say something good comes out of every disaster, and something good did. Both *West Side Story* and *Gypsy* changed because I began rehearsals with the whole company sitting around a table and reading the play—dialogue and lyrics—just as is done with straight plays. That was the first time that had ever been done with *West Side Story*. Acting became as important as dancing and singing. That changed how musicals are done, and it changed me. I re-examined my own work, I re-examined how musicals were directed, I loved directing them as I never had before.

This is clearly a memoir about change. But I don't want to just talk about change, especially how I have changed. You have seen some of that in this chapter; you know who I am today. But I want you to see me as I was and then witness the changing. To accomplish that, each of the following chapters is going to be written from the perspective I had when the events took place. The next chapter will, in all likelihood, contradict me, who I am today, what I said in this chapter. The chapter after that may well contradict both, present a very different man in the next after that. That's what change does: it changes your perspective. It changed mine and me. Watch.

TWO

Changing Changes

Looking back *(from early in 2009)*, I see that even as an adolescent, I was careening through life, not examining, not questioning, just doing. Changes in how I lived, what I did, were constant and quick, one tumbling after another; any change in me was rare and minor. In those days, I was unaware of any reason to change: we were what we were and I enjoyed careening.

Along the way, I met more than my share of famous people, even extraordinary people, who included me in their lives. What most of these people had accomplished was impressive; what some of them were as men and women was impressive; my life had to be changed by them and it was. Not me, though. Nor by events that should have changed me.

I lived in Paris for almost two years because I'd been blacklisted in Hollywood—not a small change in the calendar of anyone's days, but mine? With one important exception whose importance I finessed—an indefinable relationship with Lena Horne—I careened in Paris more or less as I had in New York and Hollywood without realizing that was what I was doing.

"The Lady and Her Musical": *Lena, the beauty who inspired* Hallelujah, Baby!

Original Story By *brought Lena back into my life. We hadn't been in touch since she walked out on* Hallelujah, Baby!, *which I had written for her. But she read the memoir and called me. "I hadn't realized how happy I was back then in Paris," she said. To make her happy made me happy.*

I made her happy once again early this summer, so much so she actually laughed. She was a recluse, confined to her bed, her vision poor, everything close to not working. But she laughed and I was so happy.

November 19, 1965

Dear Lena,

I told Steve the idea for the show and,
of course, he is crazy about it and would
love to do it. But he wants to do both
music and lyrics.

I, of course, would love to have him on
the show because he is marvelous to work
with and has marvelous ideas - in addition
to being so talented. He asked if you
would listen to the demo records of WHISTLE,
and particularly FORUM. I say "particularly"
because FORUM has what could be called
Jule Styne songs. Not all of them were
used in the show because the people
involved could not sing too well.

Please listen to them carefully and as
soon as you can and call me immediately
and let me know your honest reaction.
These are the only copies of the demos
in existence so take good care of them
and as soon as you are finished I will
have Dottie pick them up.

Love,

Arthur Laurents

dp
encs

"Best Laid Plans": *Three letters (above, and following pages) chronicling the stages of a new musical,* Hallelujah Baby!: *Arthur's first proposal, his desperate plea for an explanation of Lena's walkout, and her somewhat elusive response. The real reason? Arthur told me he swore never to reveal Lena's final and real explanation.*

Jan. 29

Dear Lena,

The show origiinally intended for you is finally going
into rehearsal. Getting it there has been the most difficult and agonizing theatre experience any of us has
ever had.

There's a shamefully long list of people who committed
themselves and then failed to honor their own committments;
of record companies who were wild about the score but
would not touch the album; of producers and investors who
raved about the book and the score but would not touch
the show. The reason was always the same: the subject
matter (and the lack of star insurance). Too many people
want to stay clear of the race issue and are convinced that
audiences will do the same. At one stage, there was the further obstacle of a whispering campaign among Negroes that
the show was anti-Negro. Fortunatelyy all we had to do was
allow the books to be read and that was that.

Somehow, during all the agony, we managed to keep re-writing
and polishing and making the material better and better and
still better. Even now, however, we must face the fact that
no matter how good the material may or may bot be, the subject matter is anathema to many ordinary people as well as
to extremists on both sides who want it treated their way
only. Still, there are people we picked up along the way -
actors, producers, director, choreographer, designer, investors, etc. - whose love for the show and whose belief in
it is monumentally heart-warming.

All the headache, of course, began with you. For years, you
asked me to write a show for you. When I came up with the
idea for this one, you (and your apparent mentor, Jean Noble)
were excited, even thrilled. You wanted certain people; I
got them. You committed yourself - and then, without reading
a word or hearing a note, you walked out. At first, you said
you were having a nervous breakdown. I believed this, in
part because you said it and in part because you had just
indulged in an anti-Semitic outburst at my house before strangers.
You said you had to go away for a rest under doctor's care -
but you went to London to make an album. Then you said you
didn't have the physical strength for 8 performances a week -
but you played Las Vegas and Reno seven nights (and, curiously
enough, the Catskills). And then you said you needed an
operation on your foot - but never asked that the show be
postponed til you were better. You just walked out.

-2-

And you and Ralph Harris wrote my stunned collaborators letters which were full of distortions, mis-
representations, even - in Harris's letter - flat lies;
letters which tried to drive a wedge between my collaborators and me; letters which never once said "I'm
sorry", not even out of politeness. And never a letter,
a note, a telephone call to me. Fifteen years of a
relationship I treasured - walked over and tossed out.

Why?

I won't say you have to give me an explanation because
I know how difficult it is for you to give anything.
But I have absolutely nothing material to gain from
your answer, so you can relax. I simply would like
to know the real reason for your strange behavior
in the hope that something, some part of those fifteen
years might possibly be salvaged.

                    Sincerely,

Jan 5 / 67

Arthur,

So glad your show is finally on the
move - I never of course doubted for a
moment that something as good as you
think it is, would ~~~~ be done. I never
read the script, but knowing what a
perfectionist you are, I'm sure that you
have done your best to make it absolutely
great!

I am just home from a long, +
painful stay at University Hospital, and
will not be able to be about for 2 months
or so. I'm still in a great deal of pain
+ have neither the strength, or desire to
make up some sort of explanation that
would please you. I admire you and
still love you, and wish you well.

                    Lena

A few weeks later, when she died, friends called to commiserate. But the morning after, I had called Gail Buckley, her daughter. Gail is lovely and much loved with a kind of humorous serenity. She was calm on the phone: it was time, Lena had wanted to go. Without seeing Lena—she kept putting me off, even, near the end, asking me, through Gail, who was always there, always the go-between, to call back another time—I felt this very complex woman was ready to go. Life had disappointed her; she'd had enough of it.

I asked Gail if there would be a memorial. Sentimentality is not for the Gail Horne Buckley who wrote a very clear-eyed, very good book about her family. "Not if it depends on me," she said. "Memorials are where everyone talks about themselves."

When I left Paris and came back to New York, I had my first real hit in the theatre, *The Time of the Cuckoo*. Life changed and I suppose I did, a little anyway, but neither change was what I had expected. Some money came, but money never meant that much to me. I never had champagne tastes; I was confident I would always make enough to pay the rent. I never wanted celebrity, the opposite actually, and largely succeeded. The change I did expect from that first hit, what I wanted from it, I didn't know then. Getting it changed me, and *that* changed everything for the rest of my life.

I can't fathom what I meant by that wild overstatement. The Time of the Cuckoo was a moderate success that gave me moderate standing in the theatre—a small change for that moment. The one real change it made in my life was earning me enough money to build the house on the beach in Quogue that is still home for me today.

I had it, I recognized I had it, and I held on to it. I was alive, exclamation point. I knew it the moment I was—unforgettable, that feeling. I should have bottled it: mortals are mortal. Change came again. It always comes. If it's good, it's easy to be open to it. But it isn't always easy; there are also those moments when change can make you question being alive without the exclamation point.

Change comes to each of us at a different tempo. Mine came slowly, reluctantly before the marvel of a change that hit me when I wasn't looking—which, of course, is just when that change does come, the difficulty being that we're almost always looking, even if it's through the slits between the fingers of the hand over our eyes. I floated on that cloud a long, lovely while. Then the wallop that almost knocked me out. Well and good to be careful crossing streets, but the car can jump the curb and run you over on the sidewalk. It changed me. It's still at work, like the aftershocks of an earthquake.

It wasn't easy for me to keep up with the inevitable changes that accompany going into the not at all brave new world of the army. Not that I really tried. What I wrote about that period in *Original Story By* was true enough, but, reflecting how I was living at the time, the book veered from one anecdotal event to another, skimming over one change or another without realizing how much each influenced where I was heading because none changed me.

I was drafted before we were at war and didn't get out of my enlisted man's uniform until five years later, without ever having been overseas. If I said I felt guilty, and I don't think I did, it would have been pretense.

Nonsense and *pretense: a foolish attempt to display my vaunted honesty. Of course I felt guilty. All three of us in the unit the army formed to broadcast a propaganda series for the home front called* Assignment Home *felt guilty. There was an attempt to go overseas that failed because such an excursion was only for officers.*

We boasted two in our unit: a colonel who directed the show and a captain who did research for me and typed the scripts. I was a sergeant who wrote the show. My superiors could have had me appointed warrant officer but saw no reason to until it was too late. The little colonel—and he was little, shorter than I and I was under 5' 8"—finagled his way onto a plane that flew over a South Pacific War zone and got himself a combat ribbon. Proof of his exposure to danger was his impotence when he came home to New York and his six-foot WAC girl friend. He was a good director, though, and a very smart infighter.

One of the last radio propaganda plays I wrote for the series was The Knife. *It dealt frankly with racial prejudice in the armed forces and, by extension, in the nation. Even the broadcasting network was excited about it. Suddenly it was canceled: the generals had gotten advance word that the war in Europe was ending, V-E Day was coming. It was back to the back of the bus.*

The little colonel was damned if some uniformed assholes—he always wore his—were going to prevent his play from being aired. He got to the Secretary of War, Henry Stimson. Stimson read the play, ordered the play to be aired, then gave us a citation for it. Would that it was he was in power today, not Robert Gates.

Except for a few moments while I was still in uniform, I felt lucky that I hadn't been overseas. Today, I know I was. Today, I'm ninety-two; then I was twenty-two. Today, day after every day—I've lost count of the years—I see what happens to those young reasons for yellow ribbons around trees and patriotic flags in windows, those boys and girls sent needlessly to Iraq and Afghanistan who don't ever really come back. Today, I feel guilty because I feel complicit in letting our elected leaders destroy lives because it keeps them alive politically.

Not long before I was inducted, there was a change of sufficient

JOHN EDGAR HOOVER
DIRECTOR

Federal Bureau of Investigation
United States Department of Justice
Washington, D. C.

April 7, 1945

Mr. Arthur Laurents
105 West Fifty-fifth Street
New York, New York

Dear Mr. Laurents:

        I wanted you to know how happy I was with
the program last evening. I thought the script was
particularly well prepared and you did an excellent
job of getting across the points that we had in mind.

        I regretted so much that I was not in my
office on the occasion of your recent visit to the
Bureau for I would like to have said hello to you.

        I do hope that the program will accomplish
what we all have in mind.

        With best wishes and kind regards,

                                Sincerely yours,

                                J. Edgar Hoover

Strange Bedfellows: *Although politics brought them together for propaganda radio plays,*
it is just as well Hoover was out that day, as Arthur was no fan.

significance to give my careening a direction: I acquired a résumé as a writer for television. Not that I regarded myself as a writer—television didn't mean I was, any more than the movies I scripted later did. Writers wrote plays, writers wrote books; the work came from a person, not an amalgam.

That we weren't at war made me resent being drafted even more. My mother had worshipped FDR, we all did; now he was a warmonger. The army was going to end my career just as it was beginning. As it turned out, I was wrong. My career flourished in the army, faster than it might have had I not been. It began with my transfer from Fort Benning, Georgia, where I had been sent by mistake, to the army's film unit in Astoria, Queens, to write training films.

That I had only written for radio and television, that I knew nothing about writing films was simply one more snafu in the hasty assemblage of ill-fitting uniforms hopefully called an army. "Snafu" raised the intellectual status of the armed forces with arguably the most useful acronym in American history. Situation Normal All Fucked Up describes our financial system, our Congress, our whole government as accurately today as it described our army back then.

One snafu kept me at an induction center on Long Island for five weeks (in one uniform) instead of the regular two days; another sent me to Fort Monmouth in New Jersey to learn how to kill the enemy pre--Pearl Harbor with a broomstick because guns were more plentiful at the Smithsonian; a third dumped me at Fort Benning into a photographic unit just as it was being readied to ship out overseas. That I couldn't take a picture with a Brownie was rectified by anointing me a truck driver. A mishandled Brownie couldn't have hurt anyone, but a truck? I imagined myself under one.

Both potential victims and I were saved by a last-minute reprieve—the transfer to Astoria. The relief that I wasn't going to die under a truck blown up by a bomb is unforgettable. Someone had to be watching over me.

My father drove down to Fort Benning to take me to Astoria and home. The trip took two days, during which his happiness, contained as usual, was contagious. I was always happy with him, but I didn't fully appreciate the humanitarian he was until late in his life. In a way, it's better that full appreciation came late, because when it did, he knew it and it meant all the more to him. It came because I had changed, of course.

There was another trip we took, when I was about ten, my dad I and I. Just the two of us. He drove me down to Washington for a weekend to show me how the nation was what it was. He took me first to the Supreme Court—he was a lawyer *(a respected profession in those days)* and explained how it worked. Then to Congress, where

Family Pool Party: *He took care of both his parents ultimately, but his father was always his favorite.*

he explained how it was supposed to work. There was a Senator William Borah he admired, whose principles he shared, but what he most admired was that Borah didn't just vote for them, he fought for them—on the Senate floor, in his own state, and around the country. What impressed me more even then (I was an old child) was that the senator was a Republican—a contrary Republican, but he still sat on what was the wrong side of the aisle for my family, and my dad admired him anyway. I didn't tell him how much that made me love him. Boys didn't talk that way then, if they do now. If they ever did, it's not recorded in anything I've read.

My dad introduced me to the senator, and the senator pretended he knew my dad. I knew they were both pretending—a black mark in my book. I was so fucking moral. Fortunately, that me has changed and gone. I was wrong. Constituent and congressman know their parts and play them as they are meant to be played. Everyone in government does, one reason the government doesn't work anymore. The curtain has long since come down on that play.

I didn't buy the pretense. I was ten then, smart for my age but with an attitude that isn't smart at any age. Seeing events from that angle only made for misplaced cynicism. Learning that took too long, but a cynic gets a lot of laughs.

Then there I was—once again in a car, my dad driving us across the changing countryside from Fort Benning, Georgia, to Astoria, New York. He was so happy to be doing that for me, his love fueled the journey just as gas fueled the car, except he never had to stop for a refill. I inherited love from him, but until it had a human form and became the center of my life, my reason for being alive was sex.

New York in wartime was a testosterone mosh pit. Everything was rationed with the exception of alcohol, sex, and inhibitions. I more than liked alcohol, I loved sex, and I went hog wild. I discovered what sex could be; what it could be was amazingly, devouringly more than I had ever imagined.

Ten years ago, when I wrote about that in *Original Story By,* I went into too many details; I was more specific than I would be today. It was gratuitous, a how-to with examples. It wasn't that I wanted to titillate or boast; it was a blind belief in honesty that was misconceived. Sex was a jolt, an awakening, a new country I wanted to write about, and I did—too much. I wouldn't now; it doesn't interest me that way now. Not that it has lost all its interest. It hasn't, and I can't imagine it ever will. The difference is that its importance has lessened and my perspective is very different. Sex has become personal. I no longer want to write about it and share mine with anyone other than the person I have it with.

The discovery of sex, for that's what it amounted to, changed my life more than anything had before. After the war, when the party was over, that change began changing as I began to discover the importance of sex to more than the body—its influence on the mind, its involvement with the heart. When I fell in love, the change was radical. It moved sex down to second place with the heart in first. That made the acrobatics more exciting than they had ever been.

Age hasn't had the expected diminishing effect on sex for me until very recently. According to my doctor—a distinguished head of one of the finest hospitals in New York —*Michael Marin at Mt. Sinai. I went to him for his specialty: an operation on my carotid artery. He said: "I love performing that operation. I would love to perform it on you. You don't need it." He explained the technology involved in the diagnosis and then we talked. Just talked a long time about so many different subjects, about life, really. At some point, he decided he would be my internist, my doctor as we used to say. It was the best decision anyone has ever made on my behalf. I check everything from what the local doctor in Quogue says to a troubling cough. His medical knowledge is vast. Should there be something he doesn't know, he knows who does. He isn't licensed, but he's a psychiatrist. He has common sense, he makes house calls—yes, he does— and he's a friend. I will always be grateful he is in my corner.*

Now to get back to more than a year ago where I was saying that according to Marin, my active sexuality combined with my continuing creativity are why I'm noticeably physically and mentally younger than my insurable age. Sex, Marin said after completing his examination in one of those sexless hospital rooms, has a positive effect on the organs of the body and on the brain. That made me feel better morally as well. For the last three years, however, my sex life is no longer a life. It's alive but not so well. I don't think the reason is age. Since Tom died, life isn't life as I knew it, either. We're not meant to go through it alone.

Radio in the twenty-first century is largely a medium for political personalities and rockers and rappers unless you set your dial on NPR or stations that broadcast jazz or classical or whatever your music is. During the war *(World War II will always be the war to me, just as Vietnam or Iraq or Afghanistan will be the war to those who survived them more or less)* army radio propaganda programs were broadcast over the major commercial networks, happily for me because they established me as a writer. In over two years, I wrote a half-hour original play almost every week without having to stint on sex and partying. How I did it, I don't know. It apparently was no effort then; I must have been obsessed. I can see myself in the distance but I don't recognize that careener or how he managed to do it all.

Then, during the war, when I was stationed in New York and writing *Assignment Home,* as the propaganda series was called, a drunken challenge at a party grounded me. I stayed home for nine nights *at an apartment on Sutton Place that belonged to a girl who <u>had</u> gone oversees for the USO, playing the accordion* and wrote the nine scenes that comprised my first play, *Home of the Brave.* That changed where life took me more than anything had with the exception of sex. Paradoxically, the most indelible memory the play brings up has nothing to do with career or change:

I'm standing on Broadway in front of the no longer existing Astor Theatre with my father. A huge sign says *Home of the Brave* in lights, but my father is staring at one at the bottom, much smaller but in lights just as bright. That sign says: *Based on a play by Arthur Laurents.* The pride in my father's face outshines all the lights.

I said I inherited love from him. What I meant was the ability to love. Many people don't have it, but being able to love is only that. What is fantasy or daydream won't become real until you meet the person who is why you're here. Then choice becomes merely a word; you don't have it anymore and, as perhaps you feared, you never will. You just give up control and let go. I wanted love from puberty but never gave a thought to letting go. My unconscious must have recognized the inherent danger. For years, I was all control, so for years I didn't get what is the prize and the point of living.

Home of the Brave indirectly landed me in Hollywood when the whole town, like most of its inhabitants, was larger than life. The U.S. is a country that worships stars even above money; in the late forties, the stars were movie stars who were Movie Stars. No blue jeans.

Everyone was a movie star or wanted to be a movie star or had

Matinee Idol: *Arthur fell in love with the silver screen lover,*
but not with the Hollywood lifestyle.

been a movie star or knew a movie star or knew a cousin of a movie star or worked for a movie star or waited on a movie star or wanted to have sex with a movie star or was a movie star who had sex with the newest movie star. While I was living with one, I became accustomed to the phone calls from a Star who hadn't had my star and wanted him, often for a threesome. Not with me, though. If I answered, I could hear the disappointment—I wasn't a star. Writers weren't stars then or now, either. Unless they also direct.

From when I was a kid, I went to the movies to see the Stars. *Let Us Be Gay* with Norma Shearer leaps into my mind because its title was the secret code used by another kid down the block and me when we wanted sex. Very avant-garde, we were. Years later, in my late twenties, when there were dozens of Stars as opposed to today's paltry four or five in blue jeans, I careened among them in Hollywood like an Alice in Wonderland.

At a dinner party at the Malibu house duplicated in *Mildred Pierce,* I escorted the most beautiful woman I had ever seen—Norma Shearer, no less—to her table on a deck overlooking the Pacific that was shielded by a ceiling of midnight-blue cellophane. A violinist fiddled romantically among the tables, the only fiddling going on. It was an A+ party. Hollywood as imagined in Brooklyn.

At a B+ at the picket-fence home of a pair of natural blond newlyweds, the lights were dimmed after dinner and everyone took off their clothes. I went home.

Home was part of a starless group gathered around a baby grand in a saltbox house on the wrong side of Doheny Drive singing Sol Chaplin's MGM arrangement of "Get Happy" before Judy Garland did, with Sol at the piano; I played tennis with Charlie Chaplin and sometimes continued the game by debating our respective idiosyncratic politics in his tennis house; I had dinner with Alfred Hitchcock and his family, which often included Ingrid Bergman and Cary Grant, who told me he had thrown pebbles at my window the night before (he hadn't, but he liked to make everyone feel wanted); I was part of a Marxist study group that included Movie Stars who didn't know who Engels or Harry Bridges were or exactly what the *Wall Street Journal* was; and I fell in love with a rising young movie star *(Farley Granger)*.

My first six months in Hollywood Wonderland, events like those happened so regularly, I mistook them for real life. I was having the time of mine, one that had changed radically. Every day was a bowl of cherries, pennies from heaven, the sunny side of the street. At least, that's how it seems when I look back *a year ago; today, it's like watching an old movie in which everyone is good-looking, drives a convertible, goes to the beach, plays tennis, has fun day and night, and is completely irresponsible. In sum, a juvenile fantasy.*

At a dinner party, I'm laughing in a flirtatious conversation about Piaf with Marlene Dietrich—yes, Herself, in person, glamorous as expected but unexpectedly funny. I'm conscious it's Dietrich, yet it's merely as though I had the luck for once to find someone at those dinner parties it was fun to be with.

It's a stretch for me now to understand that was the attitude I had to all of Hollywood Wonderland then, but when I keep looking, I see why.

Joking flirtatiously with Marlene Dietrich, both conscious we were joking, that was the game. When Greer Garson—a Star but a *papier-mâché* lady—tried to play with us—well, with the Blue Angel—Dietrich gave her a slow look, turned back to me, and said: "Shall I be a gentleman or should I kick her in the ass?"

The next day a uniformed chauffeur was at my door with a

beautifully wrapped parcel. "From Miss Dietrich," he said. Piaf records from Paris.

That was Hollywood. At MGM, no one insisted I write a screenplay adapted from something I didn't like, and I got my check anyway. I drove a convertible to the beach and played charades at Gene Kelly's. Why go back to New York? This was life lived with the top down and the sun always tanning and the moon always a crescent.

But:

At an all-male pre-Christmas luncheon party at George Cukor's— I'd met him in Astoria, where, drafted by mistake, he'd directed my first training film—a photographer famous for his portraits of glamorous stars said to me with a thin-lipped smile, "Marlene likes to play with little gay boys from time to time."

That was also Hollywood. It never really rained, not New York rain; smog was creeping up Sunset Boulevard from downtown and had reached Schwab's drugstore. The charade games at the Kellys' were nastily competitive; the volleyball games in the backyard were worse. There was a battle over my credit for my first movie, *The Snake Pit*. Anatole Litvak had been like a father to me, whom I loved even though he was too busy shooting the final scene of that movie to testify and save my screen credit. Credit on a movie didn't mean anything to me anyway then. Later, when I didn't have enough credits to get supplemental insurance via the Screen Writers Guild—*Rope* wasn't a credit, either, because the company that produced it no longer existed so the film didn't exist—the *Snake Pit* credit would have meant health insurance I could have used. At the time, though, credit for that movie as a movie didn't mean anything. I had seen the dailies: the acting was either over the top or wooden, the ending was false, traveling crane shots were more important than what they were shots of—it was typical Hollywood as seen through East Coast eyes. Careening among the Movie Stars was beginning to lose its luster as bits of real life began to creep in.

I knew I didn't belong, but I didn't want to. Why, I didn't question. Or why I wasn't impressed that I was friendly with Charlie Chaplin. Or Alfred Hitchcock. How I could not be has taken all these years to understand. They were extraordinary Stars in the history of film, I was a young beginner. Friendly they were, yes, for that moment; friends, no, we never were. How could we be? Somewhere inside me, whether sitting in Charlie Chaplin's tennis house or around Alfred Hitchcock's dinner table, I must have known that.

As putative friends, Chaplin and Hitchcock were similarly bestowed with fawning and feeding and ass-kissing acolytes who served as a protective wall. Chaplin, however, from the moment I saw him was unlike any other star in Hollywood. The whole kit and caboodle, including Hitchcock, looked like themselves; he didn't. Mr. Chaplin was a friendly, genial white-haired gentleman; Charlie Chaplin was the Little Tramp who could appear for a brief, startling flash if he chose. There was a third Charlie in the press, which went after him for his politics, his sexuality—for being active when the puritanical country thought he should cease and desist because he was too fucking old for fucking—and for his stinginess. The last became legend even though its source was the customary kids and ex-wives and didn't account for the range of Charlie's idiosyncrasy: he could be wildly generous in a way that wouldn't occur to anybody else.

Bill Tilden was the world's supreme tennis player, an American hero until he got caught with a fourteen-year old pupil. When he got out of the minimum pokey, he was finished in tennis—disgraced, broke, and without an income. Charlie to the rescue (he was always and only called Charlie except by the law). He hired Tilden to give lessons to Oona and his kids on his beautiful sunken court. A suggestion, a smile, and most of us who played on the court were taking lessons, too, like it or not. Charlie paid.

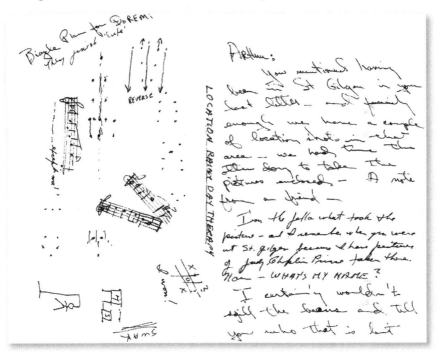

And the Mystery Guest Is . . . Charlie Chaplin: *Judy Chaplin Prince is the biggest hint; letter is from composer Marc Blitzstein.*

One afternoon, a lovely tune on Charlie's piano Pied Pipered me from the tennis to his always open main house. He was writing the music for *Limelight,* his next picture. If history was being made under my nose, Charlie didn't twig to it. I never saw him consciously being the Artist, the Subject of Biography. That afternoon with him at the piano was the one time I felt we were friends. Fellow writers? Oh, I wouldn't go that far. Charlie Chaplin is Charlie Chaplin.

He told bits of the story of the new movie to help me visualize the kind of new girl he was looking for to play opposite him. When I came back from my first trip to London, I told him about Claire Bloom, whom I'd seen on the stage. He sent for her, she got the role, and I had a miniscule part in a very small, unimportant piece of film history. Of more importance to me, Charlie behaved as though we were friends. Not buddies, not chums, but a person he acknowledged. A small change in my life for a time and then once more:

In London some years later, Charlie and Oona invited me to dinner in their suite at the Savoy with "your friend." He had begun calling Claire Bloom my "friend" in that tone too soon after shooting began. After dinner, he and Oona discreetly left us alone and eavesdropped.

"I must apologize," Claire said. "I've been very remiss. I never thanked you for recommending me to Charlie."

"Oh, you wouldn't have gotten the part if you hadn't had the talent," I said.

"You're so right," she said.

Later Charlie laughed and so did I. But actually, Claire Bloom was right. I saw that then, but I didn't ask the question that I do now, the question whose answer might make Charlie less Charlie Chaplin and more a Chaplin like Sol: why had he asked Claire Bloom to dinner with me? He didn't like her; maneuvering her to an apology couldn't have given him any real pleasure; it wasn't any kind of revenge, and if it was, for what? A performance that disappointed him?

I don't know why he gave that dinner. A friend would ask; I couldn't, we weren't friends. The temptation, the desire, the need to claim a big celebrity as yours is all too understandable. Bring it off, you've changed your life. Not just reflecting glory, you've gotten inside the circle. Except you haven't; the big celebrities value themselves too highly and take themselves too seriously to let you in. The idea is for you to keep on flattering and fawning and serving and ass-kissing while Old Man River just keeps rolling along. I like that song but I never sang it.

With Hitchcock, it was very different. From the moment he began working with me on my screenplay for *Rope,* he changed my everyday life by making me a member of his family. Daily lunch at Romanoff's at his table—my first experience of someone who had a table; weekends at his country house in Santa Rosa—he always wore a dark suit and tie. Alma, his wife; Pat, his daughter; Sidney Bernstein, his producer from the London years; they were his family and they made me feel I was. In Hollywood, in Wonderland, in that echelon, it was rare and welcome.

When Hitchcock asked me to write the screenplay for *Under Capricorn,* which would star another family member, Ingrid Bergman, I was excited. Then I read the book. I had no doubt that as a movie, it would hurt him and Ingrid as well. I didn't stop to consider how I would tell him. Hitch and I were friends; I had no choice but to be honest—tactful, diplomatic, but honest. I actually thought and believed saying what I thought would help.

Well, that me has changed. Today I'm very careful what I read, and thanks to my reputation—for once—people know what to expect: I will always say what I think or nothing. The almost universal and probably sensible custom of face-to-face bullshit followed by a behind-the-back knife has never been for me.

Stars seem so familiar that you think you know them. When Tom was still drinking, he wandered into a Westhampton bistro at happy hour, saw a friendly face, sat down and had a drink with her, then came home and was telling me about his day when he burst out laughing. "I just had a drink with Joan Crawford!" he said. I had thought I knew Hitchcock before I met him, but even when I'd known him for some months, the *Under Capricorn* episode showed I didn't. He was the Hitchcock he wanted to be, when he wanted to be. The minute I began in the negative, I became invisible. To Alfred Hitchcock, director, friendship meant doing as Alfred Hitchcock asked.

Surprisingly enough, through my agent, he offered me another screenplay: *Torn Curtain,* for Paul Newman and Julie Andrews. I wanted to give my answer face to face, but he wouldn't talk directly to me. Even if we ran into each other, a nod was the most I got. I wanted to explain why I was turning down *Torn Curtain,* that I wasn't rejecting him, that he was a great director—he wouldn't take the calls. It wasn't naïveté on my part; it was a repeat of my dad and the senator in Washington: ignorance of how the game was played.

Some years later, when I was long gone from Hollywood and living in the beach house in Quogue, my next-door neighbor invited me over for a drink with Hitch. It was odd seeing him again; he looked older, sadder, thinner. It was good to be with him, we were chatting easily—I could do that then, he could always do it—when he offered me another screenplay. I hoped; there was always the chance; and then there wasn't. He was going to direct a movie of *Topaz,* a book I'd been unable to finish. Every sensor was concentrated on not offending him, on restoring some of what we'd had. This time, he listened, let me explain at length, and accepted rejection graciously, with regret. What I didn't see then—frankly, what I haven't seen until now—was that he had asked the neighbor to invite me over because he wanted to see me as someone more than an acolyte but less than a friend whom he had been fond of. Great men don't have the capacity for friendship, just as even some ordinary people don't have the capacity for loving. What Hitchcock really was regretting was the time together that we had lost. He didn't say so, but he couldn't, he was Hitchcock. I must have sensed something like that, because I never liked him more than that day at the beach.

Hitchcock and Chaplin were rare. The actor movie stars were legion, some shining brighter than others, all more or less equal in the pretense and hypocrisy that were part of the role of Star.

On a long Labor Day weekend, I was sailing in the pacific waters off Catalina on a 125-foot yacht with a crew of eight to take care of four passengers: Katharine Hepburn, Spencer Tracy, Irene Mayer Selznick (daughter of Louis B., head of Metro-Goldwyn-Mayer; ex-wife of David O., producer of *Gone With the Wind;* and close friend—a rumored euphemism—of Hepburn's) and me. Irene hired the yacht. She was indirectly responsible for my coming to Hollywood by producing a play of mine that flopped. Guilt, a Hollywood staple, led to her penance: Vaselining my way into Wonderland's high society.

The glamour of my fellow passengers made me so nervous that for the entire three days, I was seasick. When we anchored and I swam in the sea with Hepburn, who wore green eye shadow, I stopped hoping the yacht would spring a leak and have to go back to the harbor.

On deck, Hepburn fussed over Tracy, constantly fetching a new pillow to put behind his back no different than the one she replaced. He didn't seem to notice. For all three days, he was dead drunk but contentedly so. He sat in the same chair, refused conversation, and moved only for his costar to fluff a new pillow, or to lift his glass, which one of the eight crew members was always on deck to refill.

All three days, Irene was on the phone to David O. on a yacht with Jennifer Jones, talking business, as they must have when they were married. Irene and Kate were on Dramamine but didn't offer any to dry-retching me. They pretended to be sailors born. Tracy told me about the Dramamine during the drive back to Beverly Hills in separate cars—I drove him and Irene drove Kate. In case of an accident, Tracy and the woman he loved or the world thought he loved couldn't be photographed together by the paparazzi.

Three miserable days. Nevertheless, if I said I'd spent Labor Day weekend on a 125-foot yacht with Spencer Tracy and Katharine Hepburn—which I did—the eyes of the listener turned as green as Hepburn's eye shadow and my approval rating shot skyward. Were there any Movie Stars classier than Tracy and Hepburn? Multiple Oscar winners, living legends, taken seriously as actors and applauded for their unconventional life together despite what everyone in Wonderland knew and pretended not to know.

That's still true today. Today, Hepburn and Tracy—the billing has shifted—are admired—despite; back then, Tracy and Hepburn were worshipped—despite. In that respect, they weren't unique. Stars like Dietrich, perhaps because she was European and from Christopher Isherwood's Berlin, had no closet, no pretense, no despite. But most stars had a despite the whole town knew and pretended it didn't. Much as we may like to think we know a secret, there are no secrets, certainly not your own. Even your mother knows.

The night of a triple-tent party to celebrate the wedding anniversaries of three directors—John Huston, John Negulesco, and Charles Vidor—Irene called.

"What time are you getting there?" she asked.

"I'm not going."

"Didn't you get your invitation?"

"Yes, but I'm not going."

"Nonsense. Why not?"

"I've had it, Irene."

"You can't have."

"I have."

"How can you not go?"

"How can you keep going?"

"Because tonight, I think it might happen."

It was never going to happen, but Irene was a member in good standing of Wonderland. Life in Hollywood reflected the life they saw on the screen, which reflected the life they lived. What they chose not to see was what Tracy and Hepburn typified: the pretense and hypocrisy of Wonderland. The glamour and the newness were stardust in my eyes at first, filler for letters home to Mother. But incident after incident, like the weekend on the yacht, forced me to see. I saw and left Beverly Hills to go back to where I had begun life in Hollywood—on what was the wrong side of Doheny. My life changed: it was now the right side of Doheny.

At this point, two of the most important parts of this chapter in this story have not been told—important because each changed me as well as my life. I haven't told them because one happened simultaneously with, and one overlapped, what I've already related. Cross cutting may work in movies and books, but not in this story. If you didn't know as much as you do about the life I had and the person I was, you wouldn't know what changed. A writer needs a patient reader.

The first of the two events that changed me happened almost immediately after I arrived in Hollywood: I went into psychoanalysis. Freud is out of fashion now; the requirement for hanging out a therapist shingle is vague and anyway, sooner or later the cure will be a pill. "Meds" is in the language until the side effects cause a mental recession. Looking at others I knew and know, and at myself then and now, I'm very grateful I was analyzed.

And by Judd Marmor, a young analyst newly come to Beverly Hills. His small office was in a decidedly unfashionable section, but he knew it had to be somewhere in Beverly Hills if he was to get anywhere. He got somewhere quite fast, to the moguls, to big bucks for the fifty-minute hour, and higher—to the top. He became president of the American Psychiatric Association and used the office well. As president, he pushed the designation of homosexuality as a mental disorder off the register. I kvelled.

At my first session with Marmor, when I said I was there because I was uneasy with my homosexuality, he confessed he knew nothing about it. Then came a sentence I have never forgotten:

"I don't think it matters what you are as long as you live your life with pride and dignity."

Pride and dignity. That changed me and my life. At the moment he said that phrase, I realized he resembled my father. Yes; I'm smiling, too. Judd's gone, but I look at a picture of him now and I still think he looks like my father.

My fifty-minute hours were learning sessions for him as well as for me. He had unusual notions for that time: he thought analysis took too long, that there was no point in digging into my childhood unless the key to some lock could only be there, that there could be group therapy—well, he was young, he hadn't become successful *yet. (Success was Eve holding out the apple to Judd Marmor: he bit and changed, not for the better as I saw it. In the late seventies, an accomplished charmer and deceiver named David Begelman was president of Columbia Pictures but had gone on a check-forging spree. Marmor, as Begelman's psychiatrist, testified in court that it was aberrant behavior. His patient was an honest man. Marmor had seen Begelman as a patient exactly once.*

I knew Begelman for the sleaze he was even before he oozed his way into Columbia Pictures. I revered Judd Marmor, I put him on a pedestal. I protested to him about his testimony; he replied it was none of my business. That upset me even more than the affair itself and continued to do so for many years.

Today, of course, I recognize not only that Judd was right, it was none of my business, but that all that did matter was what he'd done for me. What he did for himself or anyone else was his business. All that exists on the edge of my memory, anyway.

What Judd Marmor and the analytic process did for me gradually, over three years interrupted by trips to New York and one to Europe, was make me comfortable with my sexuality. That was a change that made life easier, but the times didn't cooperate. Gay liberation later didn't bring as much liberation as the former plantation owners believed, either. Progress for a minority is never as much as the majority likes to believe.

No one in the Hollywood I knew cared much one way or the other. Bisexuality was very popular then; it's probably more popular today, when there's so much emancipation that next to nothing is called by its rightful name.

My love affair with Farley Granger—the second unmentioned important event—began before I met him. Lonely in the army, I went where all lonely Americans go—to the movies. High up on the silver screen was a pure-in-heart boy with a beautiful, innocent face. Like a good American boy, I fell for him.

We became lovers shortly after I arrived in Hollywood and was subletting the saltbox on the wrong side of Doheny Drive. I don't believe in the long or short arm of coincidence, but the owners of the saltbox turned out to be Farley's best friends, and their name was Chaplin—not Charlie and Oona, that would have been too much, but Sol and Ethel. They were in the East with a musical Sol had written with Comden and Green. When I heard it was opening in Philadelphia, I began looking for a new place to rent. Philadelphia has been synonymous with disaster in my career. And with Solly's. His show died there and back he and Ethel came with ten-year-old daughter Judy, who was smarter than both of them, and out I went.

I found a small house on Lookout Mountain Road in Laurel Canyon with a fireplace open front and back in the middle of the living-dining room. Robert Mitchum lived up the street and was excitingly arrested for smoking pot. Farley helped me move in and while he was at it, moved himself in as well.

That was a big change in my life, a smaller one in me. For the first time, I was living with someone and that someone was a man. That didn't leave much room to pretend I wasn't what I was.

While I was living in the saltbox, we socialized—today, hung out—at Gene Kelly's house on Rodeo Drive in Beverly Hills, but a Beverly Hills much less grand than Irene Selznick's or George Cukor's or Kate Hepburn's. The living room had a shag rug; most of those who sat on it were young actors or directors and an occasional star, but no Stars other than Gene. Farley and I were the only open homosexuals, and we weren't open.

After the move to Laurel Canyon, we became part of the group at the Chaplins', who had become my best friends, too. Mainly writers sat on their shag rug, no one who wasn't left-wing. Except Larry Kert, the first Tony in *West Side Story*. No one could have seen that coming, not when he was at the Chaplins' to try out his new act, the HiLo's (sic) during which laughing Larry did a high back flip on the shag rug, barely missing the low ceiling.

It was Larry's sister, Anita Ellis, who introduced him to the Chaplins and Sol's piano. An incredible jazz singer who became a legend, she had her own radio show, took philosophy courses at UCLA, and, to complete the attraction, had an incredible body. There was no pretense: she knew my sexuality without being told and I didn't pretend, to myself either, that I was bisexual. We began an affair that was on and off for years, equally enjoyable, available and undemanding for each of us. Relationships like that, and I've had a long one with a man as well, are as rare as love but no substitute. Nothing is.

Original Story By covered my life with Farley extensively—too extensively, with gratuitous sexual details and unnecessary little disclosures. Memory is biased. None of us is a Proust, existing in a corked roomful of memories. Farley and I weren't friendly when I wrote my tell-all. Today we are. Moreover, in the last two years, even in the past year, the past months, I have changed a good deal. Looking back from this vantage point, I see us differently—as that first attempt at love that seems to be a requisite for the second that is love. With him, however, I wound up where I did belong in Hollywood—with people who saw movies in theaters, who ate tuna casserole, who read books and the *New York Times*, who were political and on the left. Home.

Most of them, I assumed, were in the Communist Party, an

assumption I see now was self-contradictory. They must have known Farley and I were lovers, but homosexuals were anathema to the Party. On the other hand, since none of them ever openly acknowledged being in the Party, I didn't really know they were. Then again, Farley and I didn't say we were lovers, either. So there was pretense on the wrong side of Doheny, too. At that time, pretense was inevitable with sexuality, but in Beverly Hills, it characterized whole lives.

The house on Doheny became a pit stop during the Hollywood Witch Hunt—a time when I was happiest. Well, I was. It was exciting, unambiguous—good guys vs. bad guys; I was involved, I knew what I stood for and worked for it, speaking everywhere, writing short plays, raising money for the families of the Hollywood Ten. I forayed into my former haunts in Beverly Hills in search of money but came out with comic relief from the wreckage.

Before a luncheon at George Cukor's, I overheard Hepburn explaining Communism to Fanny Brice in George's elegant garden.

"You have to share everything," Kate concluded her lecture.

"Oh, I understand that," Fanny said. "What I want to know is do I get to keep my jewelry?'

At the luncheon, I mentioned the Washington hearings underway before the House Un-American Activities Committee. The tide at the table was running in favor of the Friendly Witnesses and the Informers when Constance Collier, a middle-aged, very English actress and coach for Hepburn, gave her verdict in an intimidating basso: "Any man who repeats what a guest said in his house is a cad." Discussion over.

The Hollywood Witch Hunt is a moment of shame in American history. It roiled in me for years afterwards. I released some of

Arthur Laurents

September 30, 2002

Dear Barbra,

It's wonderful that you not only sang but spoke out and so tellingly. I think most of us underestimated Bush: he is very dangerous. An intelligent man has doubts: he has none. The country is in danger of igniting nuclear war in the Middle East and economic ruin at home but he truly believes he is leading us to Christian salvation. Oy!

The question no one seems to have an answer for is Why do most Americans approve of Bush? Yes, the Democrats have been mired in political polling and plotting and not following their consciences, but I don't believe that is the real answer. Are the American people that stupid? That ignorant? Don't answer either of those. If the Republicans win back the Senate, we will really have an extreme right wing government which will pack the courts with the kind of judges who stole the election.

It's depressing but I keep hoping that the Democrats will somehow win the election – which could turn everything around. If it happens, you will have done more than your share for which I, like so many others, am very grateful.

From the time Arthur wrote the heroine of The Way We Were *for Streisand, right up until his death, their mutual passion for politics was one of the reasons he admired Barbra.*

the anger by writing about it in a movie, *The Way We Were,* more thoroughly in a play, *Jolson Sings Again,* and finally in *Original Story By*—finally, because with the election of George Bush and Dick Cheney, the witch hunt lost its hold on me. The injustices committed every day by the Bush government made the injustice of the House Un-American Activities Committee seem like a small-town misdemeanor compared to national homicides.

When I look back now at California and informing and betrayal, it's without anger. Memory of the devastation and destruction, personal and professional, has to be nudged. Being blacklisted and the long battle to get a passport come back but with little or no emotion, more like a curiosity, a period anecdote. I can bring up one of the Hollywood Ten at a fund-raiser for their families, saying, "How do I tell my kids their father is going to prison for what he thinks?"—but it sounds agitprop, written today. It wasn't, it was valid. How did the fathers explain to their kids? But how do fathers explain today why they don't have jobs or how they lost the house or why they just sit? How do fathers explain, period?

One holdover remains from that Time of the Toad, as Dalton Trumbo called it: a deep dislike of informers that can still turn into anger.

It began with a woman I thought I knew well appearing in Washington before the Un-American Activities Committee as a Friendly Witness, a.k.a. informer. It was a very small world indeed. She named an actor *(George Tyne, whom everyone called Buddy)* who later gave Ethel Chaplin the physical reason she had been waiting for to divorce Sol. When the pair and daughter Judy set sail for Europe where he could find work, Farley and I joined them for our first trip abroad. That put informing on hold until personal contact brought out the anger. That was some years later, after Hollywood, after Farley, after Judd Marmor. It was the McCarthy era, and Jerry Robbins and Gadge Kazin were the informers who made me angry.

My adult life can be divided into Before and After the month of August, 1955. Where was I? Back in Hollywood, back where I had begun—at MGM, writing a new version of the old Garbo film, *The Painted Veil*, for Ava Gardner and money.

The royalties from *The Time of the Cuckoo* were gone, but they had bought me what I had long wanted: a house on the beach that was home and still is. Everything around it has changed a great deal over more than half a century—trees and bushes of Rosa rugosa more abundant than the dune grass, more and bigger houses down Dune Road—but my house has hardly changed at all. A new bank of windows on the ocean wall of the living room to replace the eroded old ones; a bay window in what no longer is the guest room because there is none—a one-room-bath-and-kitchenette cottage attached to the garage takes care of the very rare guest. The house is for me and my memories. It's my haven and my sanctuary.

Buying the land, five acres from ocean to bay, and building the house, small as it is, emptied the bank account, sending me back to Hollywood, but it was worth it to me. I had no idea how worth it was until that month, August 1955, in Hollywood. Both my public life and my private life changed so much that I myself finally changed and have never regressed. It wasn't Hollywood that effected the change, but it wasn't accidental it was in Hollywood. Nothing about it was accidental or coincidence. *There are no accidents or coincidences.* A person was central to both changes. It's always a person; life is what happens to people.

I was staying where New Yorkers stayed—at the Chateau Marmont on Sunset Boulevard. Lenny Bernstein, on a conducting tour, was staying in style at the Beverly Hills Hotel. He invited me to lunch. I brought a bathing suit; I knew it would be by the pool, where the waiters and the cabana boys were attractive and available. But the boys were ignored. Sitting by the pool, our legs dangling in the water, drinking something expensive—the contrast went unnoticed—we talked seriously about the riots the night before in downtown Los Angeles. Chicano gangs vs. Angelos. Juvenile delinquency was the headline around the country. Accident/coincidence or inevitable, there it was; Lenny and I laughed with joy.

Montgomery Clift had suggested a contemporary *Romeo and Juliet* as the subject for a musical to Jerry Robbins in 1949; they were friends or more. It was to take place on New York's Lower East Side during Easter/Passover, and one of the lovers was to be Jewish, the other Catholic. A hyper Jerry offered the project to Lenny and me; we flirted but declined for different reasons. Jerry kept bringing it up over the years but never with a replacement for the Montague-Capulet feud that was the stumbling block for me. Then, in August 1955, talking with Lenny Bernstein at the Beverly Hills Hotel pool about the gang riots in downtown Los Angeles, I found the replacement: rival gangs of juvenile delinquents, kids who were bigoted killers.

I was eager to write a musical with Lenny and work with Jerry. Lenny loved Latin American music. I didn't know Olvera Street and Mexican Los Angeles, but I did know Spanish Harlem. We called Jerry; what had been *East Side Story* was now *West Side Story*. Jerry was ecstatic. He would have been if it had been *The Beijing Story*. Lenny was going back to New York, but Jerry was coming out to do *The King and I* in the movies. I could work on the story and plan with one, then the other until all three of us were back in New York and around the cauldron together. *West Side Story* was underway.

The change *West Side Story* made to my career and my life didn't come with opening night; life doesn't imitate soap opera. It took quite a while in coming, but when it came, it was huge. It didn't, however, change me; it couldn't. I had already changed. Even before *West Side* went into rehearsal, there was a monumental change, the biggest I would ever have in my life. I had fallen in love. What that was like is indescribable. A new me in a new world? Well, I got bigger and my world got smaller. I cared about him, us, my work, and the loving friends who now loved him, too. I knew what happiness was. Nirvana.

It's Gore Vidal I have to thank. Present tense. I will always thank him. He was at MGM, too, probably writing for himself, certainly for money. We had known each other back East; we knew we had different views sexually. Gore deplored that mine hadn't changed.

"Typically homosexual," he sighed in despair. "A romantic seeking an affair." Actually, I had come to the Coast in pursuit of an affair that ended before it began. The moment my would-be walked into my place at the Chateau Marmont, I knew instantly, the way you do, that he wouldn't be and gave up on him and any romance for the duration.

"I have the perfect mate for you," Gore went on. "A would-be actor. His name is Tom Hatcher. You can find him at William B. Riley."

Why not? Romance may have been out, but sex, *pace* Gore, wasn't.

William B. Riley was the best men's store in Beverly Hills; Tom was managing it. He was more than handsome; I saw that, but it wasn't what attracted me to him. His whole life, everyone could see that, but it wasn't what attracted them to him. There was a look in his eyes, that mischievous twinkle and his available heart, surprising intelligence—surprising because it wasn't fair that anyone who looked like that would have brains—but most of all, a look that made you want him to like you. For me, the first attraction was his mouth; for him, my forearms. Figure that out.

I introduced myself as a friend of Gore Vidal's. That brought the twinkle and a grin and he said, "That man of letters." That did it: a shared perception, a shared laugh.

That day was August 24, 1955, his birthday. I can see his face and hear his voice in the moment we met today. We were together for fifty-two years. He died of lung cancer on October 26, 2006. I am still figuring out how to love without him. Thus far, I haven't had much success.

On public television, a writer was interviewed about the book he had written about the premature death of his adult daughter. Before writing, he had asked his friend, the editor of the *New Yorker*, for

At Long Last, Love: *The young man from Oklahoma would forever change Arthur's life.*

Young Leading Man: *Tom joined Jane Fonda and James MacArthur in Invitation to a March.*

advice. The editor advised he write with grace, not pain. "Grace, not pain," the interviewer repeated, "how lovely."

It is lovely. Very *New Yorker*. It brought to mind reading a piece in the magazine and wishing it had blood in its veins or an erection or would just vomit. With grace, of course. And a sense of humor, that's essential. And irony. Be careful, though. Too much humor or too much irony can freeze the blood in the veins, deflate the erection, or just end it all with a burp.

Tom was born in Ada, Oklahoma, and bred in Tulsa, an eastern city; twelve years younger than New York--smart me but wiser, more mature, more worldly. At the outset, he said it would be a mistake to try to emulate a heterosexual couple and play roles. He also said man wasn't monogamous. Years later, in his swimming pool in Quogue, a Turkish woman who looked like a Californian, a great friend to each of us and both of us (*Cigdem Onat, great teacher, great actress and director, deeply spiritual and philosophical and funny, one of my beloved friends*), asked me what our secret was, what had kept us together for so long. My answer, she reminded me recently, had been: "Permission." That had come from Tom.

East Meets West: *The Turkish actress Cigdem Onat became a close friend and collaborator.*

Everything, for me, came from him. That August when we met, there was a heat wave. We would drive in a convertible through the soup of Santa Monica Canyon down to a restaurant-bar at the beach. One night, he said, "You don't know it, but you're in love with me." I was terrified; I was a control freak; I knew he was right. I was in love with him, we were in love. All my talk about sex, I never had sex with anyone like sex with him, and he was blond. I never had a cup of coffee with anyone like coffee with him. Love is a magician. I changed, my life changed, the world changed. Tom Hatcher was the best thing that ever happened to me and still is, even though he's dead. For which I blame Sloan-Kettering.

That's an encapsulation; it didn't happen that fast. There was never any going back, although there was that once we seemed to be washed up. Change was incremental: we were marvelous, then not; high-low was the pattern for half our years together. We must have been meant to be together, because we stayed together, and in the eighties, he went into AA and we grabbed the brass ring. From then on, we got better and better and better until we couldn't get any better.

After that drive down Santa Monica Canyon, he took me to his good friend, Christopher Isherwood, for approval. Christopher's great, honking gulps of laughter took him off the bookshelves. I passed muster and we became friends. I took Tom to my good friends, an anthropologist who also "took from" Judd Marmor, as a mutual friend put it, and her screenwriter husband. They talked about Farley.

I was finished at MGM. Ava Gardner preferred her bullfighter in Spain to *The Painted Veil*, the studio replaced her with Eleanor Parker, I quit. Sometimes, things fall in place as though there were a God who favored lovers.

Jerry Robbins arrived to choreograph *The King and I* for Fox but wanting very much to talk with me about our musical *Romeo and Juliet*. There was a guest room in his grand rented house in Beverly Hills. When Jerry met Tom, he adored him, he adored us, he insisted I move in. I wouldn't have to go back to New York; I could stay on and be with Tom. I moved in.

I'd never seen a Jerry like that. Tom changed him. Or Tom with me changed him. He was caring, he was affectionate, he loved having us in his house and we loved being there with him. I had never seen him so happy; I had never been so happy with him. It was unexpected, startling even, that one person, a recent arrival in our tight-knit world, could bring both of us closer than we had ever been.

Tom may not have been aware of his looks *(He was the least vain person I have ever known.)* but he was well aware how the openness of his face enabled him to make totally outrageous statements and be totally believed. After more than half a century, even though I knew better, I believed him every time right up to the end. He suckered me until he lost the energy to smile.

In New York, we lived openly together and didn't think about it. That was how we wanted to live, that's how we would live. We didn't work out how we were going to live, there was no need to. It was so wonderful living together and being together, we thought that was what life was about, i.e., love. That *is* what life's about, but I think you must have it, then lose it, then get it back to fully appreciate it.

People were welcoming early on and for a time. Tom read Tony at the *West Side Story* auditions, which made Lenny lament that Tom couldn't sing, he was so perfect for the role. His wife, Felicia, was lovely to Tom because she knew Lenny didn't lust for him and didn't go for blonds anyway. They both welcomed us; Nora Kaye, my almost wife, welcomed us—she liked drinking with Tom. Bill Inge said, "How does Arthur get them?" I took it as a compliment. The beginning is always glorious, the early time is safe, there's no need to be alert.

In the gay world, we were fine because of Tom's looks and I was secure in his love. But we didn't spend much time in the gay world, and the straight world was beginning to make Tom uneasy. I had a presence, he didn't. Husbands and wives and lovers get short shrift; a gay lover gets no shrift. In my play *Two Lives,* the character who is me says about the character who is Tom, "They would ask him to fetch them a drink and when he came back, they wouldn't be there."

He loved the theatre. His knowledge was wide and his standards were high. He didn't think he was good enough as an actor but kept at it because he didn't know what else to do. It wouldn't have made trouble if we had talked about it, but we didn't. We didn't know then that to stop erosion, it's essential to talk. There was one moment that redeemed everything then, and bonded us some years later.

We had taken my parents to dinner and the theatre to see *She Loves Me.* As we were putting them in a taxi afterwards, my father stopped to put his arm around Tom. "I feel I have another son," he said. I couldn't stop the tears.

My father. My father loved Tom and Tom loved him. They were closer than my father and I were; he told Tom things he never told me. After my father died, Tom would let drop something he had said when I needed to know it.

My mother didn't like Tom. I brought it up one summer when my parents were living in one of Tom's houses in Quogue and he was taking such good care of them. His parents were living in another of his houses. My mother could be maddeningly honest—I was unaware of any inheritance then.

"I know you think I didn't like him because he was gay," she explained. "It wasn't that, it was because he wasn't Jewish."

I had to laugh; after a moment, so did she. Her parents were socialist atheists; she couldn't spell synagogue.

We fell short of the seven-year mark. My world of the theatre was too inhospitable to him. Not that he complained; he never voiced any unhappiness. When he was dying of lung cancer, once he said, "I don't feel so well today." Once, and that was the worst he said.

I knew he was unhappy, I knew it was because of my choices in how we lived and what we did. That made me unhappy, and being self-centered, I blamed him and we fell apart. I announced I was going to Switzerland to ski—alone. He went to California to I didn't know what.

Three months later, I knew what I had done. An affair with a gentleman farmer in England didn't distract. I had made a bad mistake. I went to California to get Tom back.

He looked wonderful, he was wonderful, but he wanted to be sure I was sure. We went surfing with his friends—knockouts every one of them. I wondered if he had had an affair with one of them, a contractor he had been working with, but only wondered, didn't resent, I was too happy with half a loaf. My first time on the surfboard, I stood up and rode the wave all the way to the beach. That was also the last time I did it. If there's a metaphor there, it's drowned in Tom's pride in the old writer in the red trunks sailing blithely over the waves onto the beach.

We went home to New York together, closer and wiser.

It was real estate—we wouldn't have guessed, nobody would

Summer Blondes: *The bevy of beauties who followed Tom everywhere.*

have—real estate that gave us a homecoming worthy of confetti. It provided Tom a way to get out of acting and the unfriendly theatre world, making his life and our life together so much happier. A big change, a double.

Nothing fazed him, including minimal experience. We had bought a landmarked Italianate brownstone in the West Village on the prettiest street in the city. As contractor, we had chosen a quasi friend who was gay and the lowest bidder, but when the money ran out, he ran. There was no limit to my impatience: "It's not worth all the trouble, let's sell it." Tom sent me to Quogue and took over—a landmark, the start of his takeover of our life and me.

What I miss and will always miss is his presence. His just being there gave me a security, a calmness, a feeling that all was well and always would be. Nothing and no one can replace that. Just the memory helps, though.

He became the contractor for the renovation, then eased into being a small contractor in New York. Next: Quogue. A fifty-room house and stable on six acres in Quogue's "golden crescent" was for sale for thirty-eight thousand dollars. He wanted to buy it. Buy it, I said. He sawed the house in half—where he learned that could be done and how to do it, I didn't ask. Our lawyer, who had told me Tom had a "brilliant head for business," had been fired by Tom for chicanery. I hadn't asked for details then, either; I had never trusted the lawyer. Based on what? I never believed there were WMDs in Iraq, because I knew George W. Bush and Dick Cheney were liars. Knew how? Instinct. Tom trusted that instinct; it had made him keep a close eye on the lawyer. It carried over into the real estate world. He'd show me a property he wanted to buy to renovate. I'd say whether or not I thought anyone would want to live there. It worked until he had his fill.

The sawed house and stable were converted into three beautifully landscaped, fully furnished houses, with swimming pools, on two acres each—and rented. He was on his way to being a real estate mogul in Quogue, better known and more respected than I was. Well, he also wasn't Jewish and drank a good deal more than I did.

The balance had changed; happiness was over the counter; and I was so much easier. Tom and Quogue.

My memory is exceptional but selective, like most people: the pleasant is readily accessible; the unpleasant hides and sometimes won't come out. Take the long view of my life with Tom and it's the life everyone who knew us, straight or gay, wanted to live. But I remember the radical change, the lift when he went into AA, and the questions pop: What was going on *before*? Why did he go into AA? When did his drinking begin? Why did he drink? I'd like to skip over the answers. I didn't have to ask the questions, but then what's the point in writing about this? The point is to show that the marvelous life we had wasn't always marvelous, that we had to change to get it and hold on to it. And even then, the unpredictable tripped us up.

His brother was a bad drunk, getting worse. He was living in a house in Quogue he had designed and Tom had built for my parents, who were gone. We threatened to throw him out, we tried whatever we could think of, which wasn't much. How do you handle someone close to you who calls, drunk as a skunk, at two in the morning from Easthampton because he's locked himself out of his car and isn't sure where it is?

We called a friend who had been in AA so long she knew Bill W. and his wife Lois. Uncharacteristically, she was curt and annoyed: she didn't have a clue what to do, she hadn't been to an AA meeting in years. (She started going again, not long after it had become chic. It was the Hamptons.)

Tom went to an alcoholism counselor who told him *he* belonged in AA. He didn't question the counselor, I think because he wanted something to change. He joined immediately, gave up smoking as well as drinking, never thought of either ever again and put his life in total turnaround.

I could simply say it was genetic and stop there. Or that we all drank too much then; perhaps he wasn't really an alcoholic. When drugging was popular, we came downstairs one morning to find a very close friend, a former water ski champion, flat out on the kitchen floor from an overdose. There were tracks between his toes; we hadn't known he shot up. Tom wasn't into drugs—drinkers rarely are—and I had a governor. Whether drinking or drugging, when I had enough, I would say goodnight and go to bed. I foolishly, stupidly thought everyone could do that.

I don't want to go into details about Tom's drinking—if you know an alcoholic, you know a version of them—but I do want to tell two small tales that were signs I should have paid attention to. If you love someone there are always signs you can see, must see and must react to and take some action.

Back in the beginning, that August of 1955 when we fell in love and were staying with Jerry Robbins, Jerry gave a party. Tom knew nobody and didn't want to be thought of as anybody's boy. He disappeared. He didn't have his car, but he had hitchhiked to his apartment in Westwood before. I got into mine and drove to his, risking getting a speeding ticket. Parked outside, there was a strange car; wanting to park inside was a man and Tom, swaying drunk. I kicked the man out. Tom and I stood there, looking helplessly at one another; at least I was looking, I didn't know whether he could see. I took him in my arms and we both cried and lived more or less happily ever after. Pretty or not, a sign I ignored.

At the time his brother was making whiskey waves, I came downstairs one morning—discovery time in the beach house apparently—and found Tom sitting at the living room coffee table, a drink in front of him, smoking and staring. He'd been driving all over the island all night, with Leona, the black giant schnauzer he loved so much, beside him. The love was requited: she was sleeping peacefully at his feet. He was lost.

Leading Man: *Tom Hatcher, Arthur's true costar.*

His real estate took care of itself. There was little or nothing for him to do with his properties; small fry new ones didn't interest him. He wanted a new project, he always wanted a project. There wasn't one, so he drank. And I ignored it.

AA was the jackpot, the brass ring, the pot of gold at the end of the rainbow. We had been together for twenty-seven what we thought were marvelous years when Tom went into AA. We didn't know what marvelous was. The next twenty-five were marvelous. He changed, I changed even more than he did—I need to even more— our lives changed.

People always read us wrong. I never called the shots, Tom did, always. He took care of me, he took care of everything, he made everything as easy as possible for me. I was a writer who never had to consider the commercial prospects of what he was writing! I never had to worry about money, to think about money, which was a blessing because I was heedless about money. I never knew how much we had or didn't have. Tom would give me a hundred dollars cash and a credit card: I was rich.

He decided where we were going and where we weren't. When we were in New York, I went here and there, he might come with me, more often not. But always, always, we ended the night together. He became an essential part of my life in the theatre—beginning with my work as a director. It was his opinion that guided me.

He came up to Boston, where preview audiences for *La Cage*

We Are What We Are: *Rehearsal conferencing with the stars Gene Barry and George Hearn looking on.*

aux Folles were even more ecstatic than they had famously been in Washington for *West Side Story*. My nervousness was somewhat relieved when he told me I should be very proud—somewhat, because I sensed a reservation. We knew each other.

"The show isn't all you want it to be," he said gently, his arm around me. "Gene Barry is lousy. That hurts the whole show."

We had wanted to fire Gene Barry in rehearsal but couldn't find a replacement. I worked hard and, I told myself, successfully. But when Tom said I hadn't succeeded, the bell rang in my gut: I had been kidding myself.

Gene wasn't entirely to blame. His material was thin, to say the most. I set about exploiting it, making every one of his formulaic, pseudo-continental "Welcome to La Cage aux Folles" announcements an aria with an emotional subtext drawn seemingly from nowhere. Use imagination and bifocals and a subtext can be found anywhere, even in *Mamma Mia*. Gene came through and the show was immeasurably improved. Thanks to Tom. A small detail? A show is comprised of small details; a crucial one can push it over the goal line.

I began reading my plays to him, scene by scene as I wrote them. He was the perfect editor for me. Knowing the way my mind worked, he knew what to say as well as how and when to say it. I came to depend on him completely. His opinion—not that of collaborators, famous colleagues, producers, reviewers—his opinion guided me. Only mine could overrule. It was freeing, like taking off all your clothes and swimming in the ocean in front of the house on the beach that was home.

Skiing became the best part of our life. Tom had skied as a boy; I didn't start until I was forty. That was at St. Anton, where we both learned the Arlsberg method: *"Élégante! Élégante!"* the instructor would cry. Tom was *élégante,* I struggled.

We skied Europe every winter with a gaggle of friends, then came back here to ski Aspen until Hollywood arrived and waitresses were tipped with vials of cocaine. The East was cold and icy, but we were skiing Killington when I had—what? An epiphany, I guess. What TV would advertise as a life-changing experience. Actually, it was.

The Hills Are Alive: *Tom and Arthur on their beloved St. Moritz slopes.*

Tyrolean Tourists: *The two young lovers hit the slopes.*

I had a bad cough, so I decided to give up smoking for the week we would be there. I had tried everything, but everything failed. Tom suggested AA's twelve steps. The first is to admit having a problem you can't handle. That was easy and a relief. On to the next step I went, but cautiously. I knew I didn't have a drop of spirituality; I could smell it coming and it did. The next step was to turn it over to G-o-d or whatever you perceive as G-o-d, a Higher Power—bullshit. I balked.

I did stop smoking and stayed stopped, really to please Tom. Even a few weeks later, when I went into rehearsal with *La Cage aux Folles* with everyone smoking and almost everyone snorting, I stayed stopped. The Higher Power concept had made an inroad, despite my being a confirmed atheist.

It was Tom. He knew more about religion than anyone, including my closest friend, David Saint, who had been a Jesuit and it showed.

Tom didn't believe in any of the versions of God, but he did believe in a Higher Power, and his serenity was visible and enviable. I went to open AA meetings with him in the Hamptons, in New York, even in London. I *wanted* spirituality, but it was too hard for me to believe in something abstract.

Tom had done the twelve steps and gone into recovery. Too many in AA never go into recovery and are just drunks. He became a big deal in his home meeting. A born caretaker, he twelve-stepped drunks with endless patience, in one case taking eight years but he got his pigeon into the AA cage. While he refused to let his life become an AA life of going to meetings and reading the Big Book, he believed in AA just as he believed in a Higher Power. None of it was a balancing act for him. He didn't have to get serenity, he was just serene.

In a way, it was maddening, but in another, it made the Higher Power concept desirable and attainable. It took two years before I got it, but when I did, I and my life went into orbit. I finally understood what was important. My love for Tom, my life with Tom, my work and a few friends, that's what was important. That's the ball game.

We traveled a lot, all over: Australia, South America, exotic places like Burma, China, Thailand, but best of all was our winter holiday every year—a week in London for theatre and friends, then three weeks of skiing in St. Moritz. Just the two of us. Same hotel, same room, same table at dinner. We read, we talked, we napped, and every day, we skied. He was the most beautiful skier. What style! It changed slightly with the shape of skis but was always graceful, elegant. He led, I followed, and skied better and better. He was proud I improved so much—that made me so happy. After the early years when St. Moritz was chic with the Italians roaring up from Milan in their

Ferraris and the Greeks arriving on the mountain in helicopters and the chalet dinner parties, we never saw anyone we knew. That was what we wanted. Just the two of us.

Tom had done all of South America except Montevideo before he died. Spanish had become a project because our housekeeper's English was a verbal paella—she came from Galicia in Spain, known as the Spanish Poland. He was so determined to be absolutely fluent, he isolated himself for two weeks in Quito in Ecuador at the best school in the world for learning Spanish.

Sometimes I went with him—to Buenos Aires, where he acquired friends who are still friends; to Bogotá, where there were also friends. Making friends was as easy as breathing for him, largely because of that quality that made everyone want to be liked by him.

I wasn't with him in Bogotá when he saw *West Side Story* in Spanish. The reaction he brought home resulted in the production I directed in New York, incorporating Spanish in both song and dialogue. I'd counted on him to do the translation and help me during rehearsal, but he died before casting had begun. Lung cancer.

He'd had colon cancer five years before. Our caretaker drove him over to Southampton Hospital for a colonoscopy and I picked him when he was finished. Over the phone, he said he was fine. In the reception hall, he looked himself, healthy and glowing, but the nurse and technician kissing him goodbye were reminding to keep his appointment and wishing him luck. Luck? The appointment was at Sloan-Kettering.

It never occurred to me for one minute that he wouldn't make it. I didn't have a clue what he would have to go through, and I don't think I fully grasped the horrors he did go through. I could see the regimen of radiation and chemo sapping every bit of energy; he lay flopped on his bed like a dishrag, unable to move, unable to keep anything down, unable to anything. None of what they did to him worked. I don't know when they knew it wouldn't. I didn't know that at centers like Sloan-Kettering the patient is a statistic in a protocol. That's numero uno.

Tom, of course, never complained, not even about the surgery, which took longer than it should have to heal. His attitude was always to give his doctors complete trust. A second opinion, a question even, would undermine his confidence. He might still be waiting for that Grand Canyon of a wound to close if a subversive nurse who had a crush on him, all the nurses did, hadn't whispered that the hospital wasn't giving him the right treatment. The wound healed quickly after the right salve and there he was, left with a distended stomach and a colostomy bag. My beautiful boy. Still beautiful, though. We bought him elegant Japanese-designed long jackets in London and went on to ski in St. Moritz. That time, it was particularly wonderful. In his jump suit, he was *élégante* as always.

Sloan-Kettering was supposed to check him every three months for five years, but they didn't. And they hadn't gotten it all anyway, as it turned out.

We were in St. Moritz when he had trouble breathing. I think now he knew then. He didn't say anything to me. He never wanted me to know, he made a point of that. The one person he told—our friend in Tom's house next door to Tom—he was clear and direct with: he wanted to live as normal a life as possible as long as he lasted and I was not to know. Not under any circumstances was I to know.

He arranged all our affairs with our accountant so there would be a smooth and complete transition with everything the same as it had

Together Wherever We Go: *A joyous* Gypsy *revival with Patti LuPone, whom Arthur called "both artist and star"; Laura Benanti, "a dream"; and Boyd Gaines, "perhaps the nicest actor in show business."*

been for me. He even arranged that I would be too busy to mourn after he was gone. Without my realizing what he was really up to, he committed me to direct Patti LuPone in *Gypsy* and the Spanglish *West Side Story* after that. Oh, there were signs for me, just as there had been signs about his drinking, but I believed every word he said, and I loved him so much it was easy to be in denial, and oh, dear God, was I! Total, complete, to the last minute. And looking back, I'm glad I was. He didn't want me to know, I didn't know.

In St. Moritz, he went to a local doctor about his breathing. The doctors there are so good, it's all in one package—the examination, the tests, the treatment, the medications. No specialists, no prescriptions, and cheaper. Tom's breathing improved so much that our skiing was at its best. I see now, though, that he pushed himself to the limit to make it the best because he knew it was the last time. It was hard for me to understand how any human being could be as generous and unselfish and giving as Tom.

When we returned home to St. Luke's Place, he went to Sloan-Kettering and they confirmed what he knew: he had lung cancer. His head doctor, often S-K's face on television and until that moment a cold fish, now had a tear in his eye when he asked if Tom blamed him: they hadn't really gotten all the cancer cells with the radiation, the chemo, and the surgery for the colon. Tom—well, of course.

The drill was chemo, the shit kicked out of him, then to Quogue, where we walked in his park, sat on the bench we regularly sat on, and talked. With the advent of summer, I would swim laps in the pool while he watched. He enjoyed that.

The chemo didn't work, so they whipped up a special made-for-Tom brew that really kicked the shit out of him. They knew even as they were destroying him that it wouldn't work, that he was a goner, but they had their protocol and he was a statistic.

From the very first time, he refused to let me go to S-K with him and talk to his doctor. I knew his beliefs about doctors and didn't want to shake his confidence. In the beginning, he also refused to take a taxi to his appointment. He wanted to walk, take the subway and walk—it kept his strength up, he believed. At night, he prodded me to go out to the theatre, have dinner with a friend, and when I got home, no matter how late, wake him. I would go into his bedroom and lie on the bed with him. Our arms around each other, we would talk quietly about where I'd been, what I'd done, about us, until he murmured he was sleepy now. A goodnight kiss and I left. That memory is dangerous for tears. Well, most of them are. Driving into the city from Quogue for the next appointment at Sloan, his brother at the wheel, Tom in front next to him, me behind him, gently massaging his neck and back. Bones covered by a layer of skin. I wouldn't guess what he weighed. When he got out of the car, I could see his stomach was no longer distended. I couldn't see he was going because I couldn't bear to.

The walks in the park got shorter; then we just sat on that bench and talked; then he couldn't make it to the bench so we sat on the couch in the living room and talked. One day, I said without thinking, "I've never been so happy and contented as I am just sitting here and talking with you." There's not a day when I'm not glad I said that, because I know he heard me. He said, "I want you to know I'm at peace." I heard, but not the meaning. I was the denial champion.

One day he said, "I don't feel so well." For Tom to say that was like anyone else saying, "Get me to the hospital." He didn't want to go, however; he had a fever but he insisted on waiting for his appointment two days later.

That time I insisted on going to the doctor with him, and he didn't object. Looking back, I'm angry at myself. What more did I need to know? He was telling me he was dying and I was deaf.

The nurse adored him. She was pissed off he hadn't come in the moment he had temperature. She lectured him while she put him on oxygen and they giggled together. The doctor was distant. When I asked why he hadn't tried surgery, he answered there were little cancerous cells floating elsewhere than in his lung. How long had he known that? His answer to that was Tom should go to the hospital for tests. Tom always said you go to a hospital to die. The patient is at the mercy of the doctor; his brother and I took him to the hospital.

He looked calm, even serene, sitting on the edge of his hospital bed in one of those blue hospital gowns. Go home, he told me—there was nothing I could do while he was taking his tests. He smiled, there was even a little of that twinkle.

"You mustn't worry," he said. "I love you and I'm at peace." We kissed and I left and I wish so much now I had stayed. I had a tendency to run away from anything uncomfortable in those days.

In the corridor, one of his doctors caught up with his brother and me. "Don't look so glum. He'll be out in the morning."

We went home to St. Luke's Place on a high, arguing whether he would live three or five years more.

Tom called twice, first for his brother, who had gone to bed. He was back in charge: he needed something done. "Let me do it for once, Tom. Please," I begged. He let me. I forget what it was, it doesn't matter, it didn't matter then either, but I was glad he allowed me to do it whatever it was. The second time he called was to say he would call in the morning to let me know what time to pick him up. We told each other we loved each other as we did every night and hung up. I called two friends to bring them up to date, reassuring them, reassuring me. I was just sitting when the phone rang—a woman from the hospital. She said she'd like to speak to Mr. Hatcher. Forgetting his brother, I said:

"Mr. Hatcher is in the hospital."

"Not that Mr. Hatcher. He died," she said. Then added: "If you want to see the body, you have to be here in an hour."

October 26, 2006.

In his room at Sloan-Kettering, he was lying on a bed in that blue hospital gown with his eyes open. They weren't that bright green;

the twinkle was gone. I lay down beside him and took his body in my arms and kissed his eyes closed and began to cry. Until a year ago, I thought I'd never stop. The tears are still there, they well up occasionally, but rarely do they fall.

I have no memory whatsoever of the three weeks after that call from the hospital. Then there I am, walking into his park in Quogue. The sight of all that green, all those shrubs and plants and flowering trees that he will never see brushed with color—a loud gasp and tears as I race blindly out of the park.

Another blank in time, then I'm in our room overlooking the Thames at the Savoy in London, then in our room at the hotel in St. Moritz to say a ski farewell. The waiters who always joked with him, the owner, the whole staff is very kind to me, which makes it a bit difficult in re tears. They're always there, ready to spill—not embarrassing to friends but would be to these folks, so I use the napkin in the dining room or my gloves in the reception hall.

Our original ski instructor at St. Moritz skis with me—Tom would have killed me if I went out alone. The Swiss Alps are another world. Pure beauty wherever you look, and the air is clean and silent. The sun is shining, the snow is perfect for our favorite runs, and the season hasn't quite begun so there aren't too many people. Besides, it's lunchtime—we always skied through lunch. My breathing is easier, I'm lighter; whatever was making me anxious is gone and one day, one perfect sunny day on snow just right for our style, there he is—skiing as only he did, right in front of me. I'm happy, I'm really happy as I follow him as I always did. He glances back and smiles. Nirvana.

When I got back to Quogue, I sat on our bench in his park and talked to him. He was there, he *is* the park. I was surprised the few close friends I told this to weren't surprised. The park was Tom for them, too.

His death made an enormous change in me, more than I realized at the time, and I keep changing; writing this has changed me. I doubt I'll ever stop. When he died—I don't like passed away; death shouldn't have a euphemism—when he died, then, everything changed radically with my way of life. For the first time in fifty-two years, I lived alone. I didn't know how to do that—the first thing every morning and the last thing every night for fifty-two years we talked to each other. I had to find a way to deal with that, but, as he planned, I was too busy directing Patti LuPone in *Gypsy* at City Center to have to deal with the time in between.

I directed the production as I had never directed any before, because I no longer gave a hoot in hell what anyone thought or said. I listened in case there was something of value, but the decision was mine, I did what I thought right. I was doing this *Gypsy* for Tom, which meant I was doing it for love, which meant it was about love. When you work like that, the company, from the top down, follows and love spills all over the stage. It was palpable in *Gypsy*, a reason the show had the audience cheering. A commercial success to boot, it moved to Broadway.

I had accomplished what I wanted, but I was emotionally drained. Death lingers. I wanted to go to Quogue and sit in his park, but I was committed to do *West Side Story*. The sunny side of that street was that it would keep me too busy to know I was living alone and question if I could. Whether to fulfill the commitment became a non-question thanks to two friends of Tom's and mine in Buenos Aires, Federico González del Pino and Fernando Masllorens. Unable to find a complete Spanish version of *West Side*, I had called them.

North Meets South: *Federico González del Pino and Fernando Masllorens*
from Buenos Aires became close friends and ultimately helped bring
about the West Side Story *revival.*

They had long wanted to do the show there, so I assumed they had
a script. They did—and the corrections were in Tom's handwriting.

It couldn't have been clearer. Tom wanted me to do the show, I
did the show.

West Side Story was more of a success than anyone expected.
Which was most welcome, since it had been very hard work, the
hardest I've ever done on a show. During the Washington tryout,
my exhausted state resulted in walking pneumonia. Not that I knew
it; I knew something was wrong but didn't have time for it. When
I finally did have time, I got so sick, I would have joined Tom as I
more than half-wanted, but my doctor *(Michael Marin)* pulled me

Writer's Retreat: *Back in 1954 the dunes of Quogue were almost empty—a perfect retreat where Arthur would write for almost sixty years.*

through. One pill did it: I slept for thirteen hours and went quite happily back to work. Keep busy was my mantra.

I've mentioned Tom's park several times. It's my center. Let me explain.

During his real estate mogul days, he bought twelve acres of land in Quogue north of the highway. North. A neighbor asked whether our desired cleaning lady was black. We didn't know. We didn't see what the neighbor saw. Well, where does she live? North of the highway. Then she's black.

The twelve acres were a jungle of scrub oak and pines, clotted and throttled by bramble and bittersweet. You couldn't walk in there or see a damn thing. Nobody wanted it. Why Tom did, I didn't know, nor do I think he did. But he must have had something in the back of his mind, because the family that owned it had twenty-three members spread all over and he had to wait for each to sign. When it was finally his, and while it was just sitting there, real estate began to boom. Land values went up, black locals sold out.

The first family to settle in Quogue was the Arches, freed slaves. Today, the main difference between north of the highway and south is that north is not totally white yet.

A local kid Tom was twelve-stepping had access to a bulldozer—his father was the biggest landscaper in town. When he began bulldozing the twelve acres, I didn't know if Tom had a vision for the land, and I'm still not sure he did. The kid went sober but died of a brain tumor after he'd finished the job.

Tom, mourning, stayed away from the land, then went back and built three new houses with pools on the perimeter to rent. I knew he was after something else. He put in two private roads, Hatcher Road to the south, Laurents Way to the north. Whatever it was he was going to do with the land—a few scattered trees—would be visible only to the houses bordering it: his three and the three backing onto it from the street. Very few people in Quogue know what's there even today. It's a park, Tom's park.

He divided it into what he called rooms, with an Alee, a Great Lawn, and flowering peach and apple trees on either side of Hatcher Road. Deeper in the park, flowering later, a cherry, a rose of Sharon. Each year, he added more: Japanese maples, weeping blue spruce, and color from forsythia, crepe myrtle, and the flowers: hydrangeas, daylilies, Dutch iris, rhododendrons. Each year a surprise as he walked me through the park: a weeping dogwood, a knoll to roll the view, burning azaleas. And here and there, benches, each perfectly placed, each different, the best because it was the one we sat on to talk. His ashes are buried in an urn to one side, mine will be buried on the other.

Garden of Eden: *The pastoral retreat where Arthur found bliss with Tom and where they both now rest beside their bench*

That's the bench I sat on when I talked to him, when I squinted my eyes so I could see him riding his mowing tractor with that battered straw hat. That's changed, I've changed—that no longer works for me, I don't talk to him, I can't. I keep changing, I keep busy, and sometimes I'm busy enough not to confront that I'm living alone, that I have no life without him. But then, because I feel his presence in the park, I come and sit on the bench. I know or think I know all that's absurd, too. Still, he *is* the park, the park is Tom, and that's a comfort.

The difficulty is knowing that the one thing in the world I really want I can't have because he's dead. All the Higher Power in the universe can't get around that. I do have a hope, though. I hope he can see me and hear me. If he does, he knows everything I say and do, which means he knows how much I miss him and how much I love him. My friends don't doubt for a moment that he does. I hope my friends are right.

I envy having that hope then. It kept me alive with possibilities; it kept Tom alive. Time and cold daylight wore that hope down and out. I replaced it with acceptance. Tom exists in photographs. When I think of him, he is standing still. Acceptance is the desirable goal, reputedly. I don't know. I'm calmer, certainly, but I am also more conscious that I am going through it alone.

THREE

Reputation

*I*t embarrasses me that as recently as a little over a year ago, I could devote a chapter of a book to the subject of the above title. A whole chapter about my reputation? A paragraph is giving it too much space. God knows I've changed on that subject. Today, I am indifferent to whatever reputation, good as well as bad, I might have in Quogue or anywhere in the world. To be sure, good is preferable to bad; bad brought anonymous telephone messages on my answering machine such as "Do you know how many people hate you?" and "Haven't you died yet?" At the time, I was upset; today, I would simply erase the voice and move on.

It's difficult to remember the me I must have been back then. But what better way to show how I've changed than letting him have his say—and saying what I think of it today?

Underway at this writing *(Spring, 2009)* is a Dramatists Guild project of filming interviews with older playwrights who discuss their work, give their views on writing for the theatre, and natter on about anything else they feel like. I don't really know whether that last is true, but it's what I did, and at length once I got going.

However worthy the project, I resisted taking part. I've been beaten up lately—me, not my work—in newspapers and glossy magazines by gossips impersonating journalists and on TV by talking empty heads, bloggers, all the usual suspects to such an extent that I didn't want to provide more fodder. When the jackals are roving, anything

Father and Son: *Arthur became my mentor, collaborator and best friend.*

one says or does, especially on unedited film, is prime meat for the pack to tear to bloody pieces.

Those filmed interviews, however, could be helpful to young writers in schools everywhere as well as a record for the Guild archives. The drill was that the old playwright would be interviewed by a young one. I didn't know one who knew me or my work; I wanted someone who did and would prod me, stimulate, provoke jokes, good and not so good, someone with whom I would have a good, informative time and therefore so would the audience—if they ever got one. In short, I wanted David Saint or no interview. So David Saint it was. Yesterday, for a brief moment, I had misgivings about that decision.

No one knows more about me and the theatre or could care more about both than David. The film begins with him talking about me, and he began by repeating a canard he had heard about me before we met. It came from his agent, who had advised David to think at least twice before accepting my offer to direct my new play.

"He eats directors alive," the agent had said.

All this was related by David with a humorous smile, but what flashed through my mind as I looked at him on the screen was that even David was unthinkingly continuing the legend that "mean" is my middle name. So? Does it matter?

An unequivocal No is the answer, but I wanted the reader to understand that the hurt can come from anywhere, even un-intentionally from someone who loves you. We have to be very careful of each other. We don't always know what will be the trigger.

With David and me, exposure of the unintentional doesn't matter, because we always talk to each other. Not joke—talk, and immediately. Lots of people talk as easily as they flirt, but how many talk out whatever has caused a momentary glitch? If you don't, the moment becomes perilously longer and longer and then you've done yourself in.

When David saw what I had written—I show him everything, as I used to show every page to Tom—he explained he had deliberately quoted his agent because he thought it would benefit me if, as my interviewer for the film, he didn't come off as a sycophant. Well, maybe. Still, he made the film a highly stimulating interview.

It's only relatively late in life that I've been deemed a target worth shooting down in print. Until then, I never gave a thought to what was said about me one way or the other. What you don't hear is like that tree falling unheard in a forest. After all, how many colleagues are going to tell you to your face that you are mean? They might tell you to your face that you're full of shit, but that would be over drinks or dinner or during intermissions. Still, what brought on the attacks, verbally or in print? Something in my behavior must have been partly responsible. My vaunted honesty?

From the time I was comfortable with my sexuality, if I believed something was true, I would say it. Much of the time, how I put it made people laugh. Elaine Stritch said it was my delivery, not what I said. She said that at a time she considered herself a friend. I considered her a friend, but, as Steve Sondheim pointed out to me, I was never too swift in that department. Elaine was validated for me because she went to AA with Tom Hatcher.

I credited AA with more than it claimed for itself because it had been so remarkable for Tom and therefore for me. Whatever was said about me, pro or con, didn't matter: he was there, it was he I heard. His opinion guided me; he protected me even when I didn't realize it.

An illustration. Ten years ago, during intermission at a performance of a musical at London's Donmar Warehouse, a respected young

English agent reminded me we had met. *(Simon Beresford was the agent.)* I vaguely remembered meeting him. *(Simon presses on just as easily without encouragement.)* He asked if I was enjoying myself.

"No."

"What do you think of So-and-so?" His client, probably.

"Not much."

Tom to the young man: "Don't let him upset you. That's just how he is."

This was said with that smile and a twinkle that was magic: we all laughed. Tom had made the young man see what he saw—not a cynic who was mean and to be feared but a man who, like Pavlov's dog, automatically said whatever he thought when asked a question and was somehow funny at the same time.

A nice introduction to Simon, who is one of the triumvirate who are my reason for visiting Brighton, a small coastal city that is as friendly as the West Village for much the same reason.

Always saying what I believed to be true may have been popular in some church I didn't go to, but it didn't make me popular. Not that I knew it; if I had, I might have changed earlier than I did. I didn't even suspect it was achieving almost the totally opposite effect, because that had only been verbalized. To register for me, it had to be in print, typeset print, not a blog. I didn't and don't read blogs; they're after my time. Blogs, websites, twitters and twatters didn't exist when the first hatchet job done on me appeared in print. That, as it happened, was in the *New York Times*.

That most distinguished newspaper in the country, in an effort to boost circulation by getting younger readers, initiated a theatre gossip column, which was akin to a middle-aged woman walking out of church to shake her booty at a downtown club. The column didn't increase circulation, nor did it last very long, but while it did, the woman who wrote it took after me during the previews of *Nick & Nora*, which I foolishly wrote and directed.

The woman obviously has a name I know and probably many of you do, too. I don't want to use it, because doing so might offend a third person with whom I have a relationship I want to keep. So I shall give her another name—Louella, Jr.—in honor of the first gossip queen I knew: Louella Parsons of Hollywood, USA.

I was seated next to Miss Parsons at a lavish dinner party Louis B. Mayer of Metro Goldwyn Mayer gave for his daughter, Irene Mayer Selznick. The party was to celebrate the success of Irene's Broadway production of A Streetcar Named Desire. *Streetcars were ubiquitous: miniatures on end tables, a huge ice sculpture the dinner table's centerpiece. Slowly, during the overlong dinner, it melted away on the double damask tablecloth.*

Miss Parsons turned to me during the fish course: "What picture are you in?"

"I'm not an actor, Miss Parsons."

She turned away and all I saw of her after that was her ample back.

Louella had real power. Stars and studios were terrified of her. At Christmas, she sent her car to collect presents from everyone on a list she gave her chauffeur. If they didn't have them wrapped and ready, looking as extravagant as they would have done in an MGM movie, the Santas knew what awaited them in her column.

As for Louella, Jr., I doubt she even has a car.

Those previews for *Nick & Nora* went on for so many weeks it felt like all four seasons; the show was begging to be attacked. And it was, and not exclusively in the Times. Hubris, not so plain and never simple, kept me involved, hubris fed by the memory of a wildly happy and successful romp I had directed and helped create called *La Cage aux Folles.*

La Cage, the first multimillion-dollar gay Broadway musical, was a dicey prospect. To me, not to Allan Carr, its producer. He came from Hollywood and the music world of the Village People. He was accustomed to hits and *La Cage aux Folles* was another, a huge one. A four-plus-year run, several road companies in the U.S., others in London and Sydney (where the ensemble in drag was straight while the crew was gay). It was beautiful to look at, all the companies were happy companies, I was happy, and a percentage of the authors' royalties everywhere, now and forever, for my contribution to the book did not make me unhappy. That contribution was rooted in my conviction that a large majority of the audience anywhere in the country (except San Francisco) was not gay-friendly. To tilt the show to play to the converted would be to close in three weeks. To broaden its appeal, I converted it to the tale of a boy who has to accept a man as his mother. Despite all the drag, it was a family show. I also made sure there was no sexuality and held camp down to a minimum.

Just about the time we went into production, something called GRID infected the gay community. Even when GRID turned into AIDS, it was largely ignored, even by the population hardest hit.

As one year, then another jazzed by at the theatre—cocaine was as prevalent as dance belts backstage—the company began to sweat out who would be the first to be struck down. It wasn't even cliché ironic that the unlucky soul was a closet case. Nobody had believed he wasn't gay, but when he went, and he went unfairly fast, everyone wished it had been true. He had been so obviously unhappy in his denied life.

He wasn't the last. A touring company was hit more than once while *La Cage* continued in New York to packed houses that were largely straight by then and, like much of the straight population, were either ignorant, in denial, or unconcerned. Not so today, but nonetheless, today there are still religions that promote abstinence and prevent the distribution of condoms, fostering ignorance. Ignorance is the most powerful of enemies and the most prevalent, and that hasn't changed.

Anyone who lived through the eighties knows the change made by AIDS. I saw it early on because of where Tom and I lived: the West Village, the exhilarating center of the gay community in that decade. Then overnight, a heart-wrenching visible change— streets that had been alive with vibrant young men emptied overnight. That emptiness haunts the West Village to this day; even the ghosts are disappearing. The gay community, subdued, has moved uptown to Chelsea to eat, drink, shop, and work out. Downtown, the pretty, tree-lined streets are now streets for older, whiter, office people. Not much spirit, not much joy. It's not unfriendly down here, but hardly as friendly as when the young gay men strolled the streets of the West Village. You can say they were cruising, and some of them were, but gays are so glad to have a neighborhood that accepts them that they are quick with a smile and "Hello." I miss them, even the kind who shouted "Outrage!" at Tom from the other side of a street because I had disparaged Ethel Merman's acting. They made the West Village special beyond the shared sexuality; they nurtured the friendly ambience that made equality alive and well and visible.

La Cage aux Folles was a personal success for me, followed by a new and very different production of *Gypsy*, this time with Tyne Daly, Jonathan Hadary, and Crista Moore. Again, a personal success; two in a row.

Curtain Up!: *Tyne Daly, whom Arthur called "great and fearless"; her Louise, the "lovely" Christa Moore; their Herbie, Jonathan Hadary, a "helluva actor"; and Jule Styne, "not just a wonderful composer but the sweetest man with whom I worked."*

Critics tend to be extravagant—their reviews much better or much worse than warranted. The reason, I think, is that sanity isn't quotable and they want to be quoted. They want their names in the ad; they want a reputation.

The first time I'd had two successes in a row—*West Side Story* and *Gypsy* in the fifties—I hadn't needed to learn that if you believe your success, you're dead. I'd learned it back then, but this was now the eighties. I'd had failures, I knew the graph of a theatre career resembled the graph of the stock market, I was wiser. So wise, I seduced myself into believing this second double success was more of an accomplishment than it was. That led me to commit Broadway suicide via *Nick & Nora*.

I had gotten involved in this musical mystery—double meaning intended—for the wrong reason: to help a former production stage manager of mine, Jim Pentecost, get the rights to the material by pretending I was going to supervise the production. Friendship is the wrong reason for doing something one doesn't believe in. Slowly but surely I got in deeper and deeper, putting one cement shoe on one foot—I became the director—and then the other foot—I became the book writer. Add an almost nonexistent collaboration with the composer and the lyricist, and suicide became the soup of the day.

Tom had been warning me; now he simply said, "Get out." I heard. I knew he was right, I knew the show was in trouble, but I convinced myself I could find a way to make it work. Make it work. Is that what I was in the theatre for?

In her Friday columns, Louella, Jr., made allegations that were damaging distortions of the truth. How to deal with them, I didn't know. Write a letter to the Times?

What was going on in the real world at that time, I didn't know either. Every week, I read the Friday allegations; every week, I concentrated on making one major improvement each day to *Nick & Nora*; every week, I sat on a cross at a meeting commanded by the producers during which they took turns hammering in the nails. This was done around an extra-large round table with every seat filled by literally countless producers plus my presumed collaborators, who enjoyed watching the crucifixion.

There was more but I've cut it. It all reads now as though I was trying to explain away a basic mistake I made. More the fool I: it can't be done.

When a strong effort was launched to lynch the choreographer, Tina Paul, I called Jerry Robbins and asked him to see the show. Her work with a cast of nondancers impressed him; he couldn't have done better himself. We went on to talk about the whole show. He liked it, but not as much as he felt he should have. Neither did I. Why? He didn't know; neither did I. What was the remedy? Neither of us knew.

The importance here is the absence of backbiting, bitchery, one-upmanship, celebrity, schadenfreude, hatchet jobs, everything that has nothing to do with theatre. Jerry and I hadn't been friends for years, but our shared regard for the theatre and our mutual professional respect were intact. That informed everything.

The producers didn't care what he said. He was Jerome Robbins, but they still didn't care. It was their money that had gotten the show on and attention had to be paid them.

Money isn't knowledge. Investor/producers who think otherwise are rare; most equate the amount of their investment with the value of their input. It can also be equated with the trouble some of them make. The recent *West Side Story* cost a lot of money to produce. It paid back faster than anyone had dreamed, but certain of its investors/producers kept complaining this performer should be fired, the Spanish should be eliminated, the sound was bad—the sound *was* bad, but admitting it to them would have been opening the floodgates. And what did they really want? A value for themselves that wasn't just their money.

So many of us want to be wanted for something other than the reason we are wanted. Beautiful creatures want to be wanted for their brains. There's a handy solution for all: learn how to be really good at sex. Everyone can do that.

Not true, but I believed it then. I always believed sex was more important than I do now. Is that a plus?

One last Friday column alleged that the morning after opening night, I flew off to the Caribbean to hide, leaving the cast to weather the bad reviews by themselves. There were no bad reviews for the cast to weather. The bad reviews were all for me. Everything was my fault, including the music and the lyrics.

In a way, it was all my fault. If I hadn't stubbornly forged ahead, the show would not have gotten on. Any doubt that the weekly allegations were the reason it was dead in the water before it opened was dispelled by the opening line of the Times review. *Nick & Nora*, it read, wasn't "as bad you've heard." It couldn't have been. It was pretty good by opening night. I was encouraged by the young sound board operator who bought himself a new expensive pair of skis because he believed the show had improved so much, it would have a healthy long run.

Why did that encourage me? Because I loved skiing. Not a rational reason, but skiing was an important, happy part of my life with Tom, so much is traceable to that.

I knew who had been feeding the slander to the Friday column—one of the producers and one of my collaborators. I was the director of their show; damaging me, they were damaging their own show. It's possible, of course, that they knew that but disliked me so much, they didn't care. If so, they were even nuttier than I thought. Come to think of it at this distance, they did know and they were nuttier.

At one point, I wrote Louella, Jr., and her editor a letter that included proof that a particularly attention-getting allegation was untrue. Neither answered.

A simple but important lesson to be learned. Write all the letters you want or books like this, but you will never get even a distant relation to a retraction. What you stand a better chance of getting is worse mud thrown at you with better aim. Calm your indignation, channel your violated sense of justice, toss your belief that justice will prevail into the garbage. When vilified in print, the only way to deal with it is to ignore it and get on with your life.

I should have taken my own advice and ignored the whole Nick & Nora *brouhaha. It is so forgotten now that all this was new to me as I read it a few minutes ago. It's really remarkable how unimportant what was very important can become once you get even a little perspective.*

The failure of *Nick & Nora* registered. The ugly reputation registered even more. I went to Quogue and Tom and security. It was there, waiting. The phone didn't ring; he was busy with the real estate that supported us very comfortably; it was so peaceful and quietly beautiful in his park that I relaxed. I was at ease. The newspaper and the show began to drift out of range, began to lose the importance they wouldn't have had if I hadn't let myself be caught up in the small world of names in boldface.

Tom said, "Something good comes out of everything." He never sounded like a commercial or a collection plate when he said things like that. Something good did come out of that wasted time with unpleasant people. After twelve years directing musicals, I wrote a play again. I was happy just to write "Act One, Scene One." I wrote another play the next year and the year after that, and I haven't stopped since.

Whatever effect the attacks had on me, my friends had been impervious. In Quogue, people who weren't in the theatre didn't care at all because they never read Big Apple trivia. The summer people hadn't arrived; I wasn't even sure the locals knew my most recent show had been a spectacular flop. If some did, they didn't worry about me; Tom's real estate was doing well and there was always *West Side Story*. Maybe *Gypsy*, too, but I wouldn't bet on that. The point too simple for me to see was that outside the narrow world of house seats, people thought of me what they'd always thought. That's what I had to do: think of myself as I always had. But I never stopped to look at myself. You lived, you did what you did, it worked out or it didn't. Until *Nick & Nora*, it mostly had; it would again. *That's a sort of Russian roulette. Today, a major difference, I do what I do for the enjoyment in the doing. Thus the outcome is very secondary.*

When I was in high school, a teacher graded a term paper of mine A+-, writing in the margin, "You are either a genius or the most brilliant fraud I have ever encountered." I knew she was wrong on both counts; nevertheless, I wondered whether I was a fraud. At fourteen. Fraud didn't cloud my mind again until the combined misadventure of *Nick & Nora* and the Times. The next time I wondered, it was again provoked by the Times.

A good review of my first book, *Original Story By*, was spoiled for me by the reviewer, Patricia Bosworth. She had written a very good biography of Montgomery Clift; she had also done a stint as actress, even appearing in an Off-Broadway production of my *A Clearing in the Woods*. I knew her as Patty Bosworth.

Patty Bosworth labeled me "mean" because I had come down hard on Jerry Robbins for being an informer. I don't doubt that by then I'd become oversensitive to "mean." Or that I probably exaggerated the amount of shine the knock had taken off the review. But Patty Bosworth had no business reviewing any book that dealt with informing. Her father, Bartley Crum, had been an informer, and she sympathized with him. In a praised biography, she had told his story:

he'd been a famous liberal lawyer who had informed, even on some of his own clients whom he had previously defended. That revelation had shocked a lot of people besides me. I had also been shocked by his daughter's defense of what I thought and think was indefensible. In her words, that made me "mean."

Even if I was oversensitive to the word, it seemed unfair that the Times had chosen her to review my book. It was crystal clear how opposed I was to informers; it was crystal clear how she sympathized with informers. Why assign her to review me?

That was almost ten years ago. What matters to me has changed a good deal. My values haven't. A shit is still a shit. An informer like Patricia Bosworth's father was a shit, and so was she for defending him.

"Shit" was a stronger word ten years ago. It lacks power now. When I use it, it's as in "Oh, shit!" when I've forgotten something. At least, I'm no longer annoyed by small injustices. There are too many large ones everywhere you look. Annoyance isn't enough for them. They warrant anger and they get it.

Not anymore. It's a waste of energy and pointless.

Tom was gone—lung cancer. Not as easy to write as it may read. He was gone when the habit of saying something because I believed it to be true got me into unnecessary trouble. As in the opening chapter of my second book, *Mainly on Directing: "Gypsy," "West Side Story," and Other Musicals.* The first words of the first paragraph set it up:

> "The show depends on you," Scott Rudin said. "You have the musical in your bones. Sam doesn't. You have to put it there."

* * *

The show was a projected revival of *Gypsy* starring Bernadette
Peters; the Sam was Sam Mendes, who was to direct it. He did,
I wasn't happy with the result and went into far too much detail
explaining why and where I felt Sam Mendes had gone wrong. It
was true as I saw it, but the chapter wasn't about Sam Mendes's
qualities as director of a musical or about my relationship with him.
It was about the necessity of having the musical in your bones and
what happened when a director did and when he didn't—every
director, not just Sam Mendes. But because it was Sam who didn't
have this particular musical in his bones and I couldn't put it there,
I sidetracked myself. I kept connecting the proof too many times
to Mendes, which brought on a vendetta I wasn't aware of. I had
said what I did because I believed it to be true. Honesty's ugly head

Power Couple: *Arthur felt Scott Rudin and John Barlow's real power
was not due to their considerable talents and accomplishments
but instead to "their love for one another."*

again. That it was considered hurtful to Sam, particularly by Sam and Scott, didn't occur to me any more than that it was all beside my point and unnecessary. Honesty, contrary to its reputation, is not always the best policy, as I had to learn.

Learning is good; learning can open another window. Fresh air can be invigorating. It can also give you pneumonia.

A new mudslinging Friday column arrived to feed the bloggers: Michael Riedel, gossip maven on the right-of-center tabloid, the *New York Post*. He never passed up an opportunity to damn me with praise so faint even dogs couldn't hear it. Knowing this didn't stop me from going on a theatre talk show he cohosted. Why? Because it's very difficult to get any publicity for a special niche book like *Mainly on Directing . . . Musicals*.

Riedel made no secret of his intentions. As the show went on the air, in the studio's green room, two assistants, hoping for the worst, said within hearing of my publisher's publicist that The Riedel had bluntly warned his cohost, Susan Haskins, that I was his baby. "I do all the talking about his book. I'm going to get him and don't you interrupt me," he was reported as saying.

On the air, he didn't mention Sam Mendes; he was after bigger game. In the book, I described how I had changed the way several big numbers in *Gypsy* were done; Stephen Sondheim was the lyricist. How did Steve feel about my changes, Riedel inquired with an expectant smile. "Why don't you ask Steve," I answered. Another smile, another version of the same question, same answer: "Why don't you ask Steve?" And so it went—nowhere. But the book had been mentioned, and when Riedel lost interest and allowed his cohost to take over, she talked favorably about the book. Mission accomplished.

I had learned. And didn't get pneumonia. *Would I do it today? I don't think so, but this book isn't finished, let alone published. Obama promised so much in his campaign.*

I did my plays, with one exception, at regional theatres; I was out of the Broadway spotlight. The slings and arrows didn't stop, but they were less frequent. An unexpected archer was my old friend Elaine Stritch.

I was in Quogue when she called to "make amends." Making Amends is the ninth step in AA's twelve-step recovery program. Stritch and I had worked separately at the Bay Street Theatre in Sag Harbor, run by Sybil Christopher. Sybil was a good friend from way back in London when she was married to Richard Burton. She produced one of my new plays, *My Good Name*, which was directed by David Saint, the first of our joyful collaborations *that eventually developed into a lifesaving friendship.* Sybil's Bay Street Theatre was where it began.

Stritch came to Bay Street; she was unhappy her second day. Yet it was to me she wanted to make amends. Why?

Why? Oh, because of what she had said to Sybil. What had she said to Sybil? Things she shouldn't have said and wanted me to forgive her for. What things? Oh, you know how you say things without thinking when you're upset? Well, she had told Sybil I had said things I hadn't and she needed, she really needed my forgiveness. Elaine, what did you tell Sybil I had said?

Stritch has a sometimes embarrassing need for attention. She got Sybil's by telling her I had said the Bay Street Theatre was amateur night, Sybil was an amateur producer, and she, Elaine, was making a major mistake appearing there that she would regret.

Because of Tom, I'm very pro AA, but AA or no, Stritch didn't

The company of My Good Name *at the Bay Street Theatre, which became
the first of twelve collaborations between David Saint
and Arthur (pictured on right).*

warrant being forgiven. Nor did I think it mattered to her whether I did or didn't forgive her. What did matter to me was Sybil and my friendship with her. Being Sybil, she laughed off Elaine's attention-getting inventions: Sybil knew me, she didn't believe Elaine for a minute. Or she probably didn't, but isn't there always a slight doubt? Elaine is a talented performer: her smoke is smoke that has to come from some flicker of fire. Pernicious poison, it hurts even the least vulnerable. Causing hurt is very popular, especially if the target is currently successful. In this culture, success begets venom, and venom is a best seller.

At ninety plus, once again I had two big successes in a row—revivals of *Gypsy* and *West Side Story,* each innovative in its own way and both well received by press and public. Two in a row for the third time by a man in his ninth decade made me better known than

I had ever been. Once, when I came out to make the welcoming speech at the dress rehearsal of one of the productions, the length of the applause moved me so much, my legs began to tremble, so I put a hand out to hold on to the proscenium. In the speech, I had mentioned having had a brandy at dinner for a sore throat—big laugh, but it was true. The audience, however, thought I was drunk and burst into cheers.

An old reliable: in a world that worships success, success is followed by destruction. The cheers were an open invitation to whack me. And I was whacked—at greater length and more publicly than ever.

While it was happening, I wasn't aware of any of the whacking. My mind was in another place the whole period of the new *Gypsy* and the new *West Side Story*. Tom had died shortly before that period, and I didn't quite comprehend his death. It's inexplicable how you do and don't get it. I was concentrating on how to live life alone after fifty-two years with a man twelve years younger who I never thought wouldn't be there every morning. The only solution was to keep busy.

Actually, Tom had set that up carefully. He made sure I was committed to direct Gypsy *and* West Side Story *before he died.* The point of directing both productions was to give me the feeling I was alive. It did.

I wasn't always entirely aware of everything that was going on during rehearsals and production, but because I was doing the shows for him, there was love in the work that I believe made it however good it was. It brought me more success and praise than I'd had in years. It also got me the most severe whacking I'd ever gotten.

The whacking was done by *New York,* a magazine that blended gossip with journalism; its whacker was Jesse Green, who had interviewed me for a piece he was writing for the Times on Patti LuPone, whom I was directing in *Gypsy* at New York City Center.

Pleasant, gay—he commiserated about Tom's death—Jesse had a receding hairline, a partner, and a little adopted boy, a combination certain to inspire trust. I liked Jesse and his piece in the Times.

There was no sign of the dog beneath his skin when I opened my door and welcomed him into my house to interview me for his article on *West Side Story*. One visit wasn't enough. He needed just a little more information, he wanted to report everything I wanted told about the production, could he please come back. Then just this once more. On one of those positively final farewell appearances, Jesse asked if I had changed my name, I said I had, Jesse said he was just checking; he wasn't going to waste any space on that. The moment registered only after he'd set on me like a souped-up Rottweiler.

I don't read *New York*. Someone, I can't remember who, said I'd better. It probably would have been better if I hadn't, but I did. A few sentences in, I got the tenor of the piece—Jesse hacked me to bloody pieces with glee and then shit on me for good measure with out-of-context quotes and flat-out lies. Not the usual; worse and longer.

Two things I remember. One: Mary Rodgers Guettel, who not all that long ago had relied on me to calm her tempestuous family waters, told Jesse to call her back when I was dead. Mary was always funny. When told a not-attractive friend had thrown her back out, Mary famously asked, "Why didn't she throw the rest out with it?" Jesse wasn't funny. He was gleeful, though, reporting I had changed my name. I didn't think there were many in the theatre community who didn't know I had.

Changing one's name was common for various reasons in 1937 when I graduated college to face the Depression. My reason was to get a job. It was easier to get one in advertising if one were a WASP. Everyone wanted to be a WASP, anyway, have a WASP name, look like a WASP. It made life itself easier; the American dream was a WASP dream. WASP meant white, Protestant, a straight nose and blonde. The changes necessary to make the dream come true were not to be mentioned. The ads said, "Which one is the real blonde?" It was no secret that no one in the theatre or the movies kept his or her real name, but real life was all secrets. Eyes were wrinkle-free and young supposedly because of a long rest in the mountains or the desert.

Today it's the opposite. A new and wonderful young Tony has just come into West Side Story *on Broadway. His name is Matt Shingledecker. He refused to change it to Matt Decker—a porn star's name, several pornsters said. Today, hair changes color openly and regularly; faces, male and female, not young and young, are openly and regularly Botoxed, lifted, and cranked with no comment except on the quality of the work done. Today and all the yesterdays, however, have one basic in common: the emphasis is on the external.*

It always is in this country. The internal is left largely to a variety of religions. Most people know on Sunday or its equivalent what they are supposed to be and what the rules are; few know who they are and are in touch with what they feel.

The *New York* article drew a lot of attention, not only on the Internet but in theatre water holes: restaurants, bars, and offices. Like an insatiable vampire, the magazine went slurping back for more blood. The supposed subject of the next interview to promote *West Side Story* was Karen Olivo, because she had gotten a Tony for her Anita. Three mundane kiss-ass questions and then, without a graceful lead-in: "Have you ever seen the nasty side of Arthur Laurents?"

If anyone at the magazine had recognized that Karen Olivo's performance could only have come from an unusual woman, they wouldn't have made the mistake of exposing the true objective of the interview to her. The contempt in her reply was as apparent as her intelligence. Did they consider themselves journalists? Did they think she was so stupid she couldn't see what they were stooping to do, what they wanted to use her to corroborate? Eloquently, she said everything that needed to be said to the handymen of publishers and editors who believe venom sells.

The magazine cut the interview short. *West Side's* press agent had expected the large spread a profile customarily gets; what he got was a brief squib. A press agent's life is not a happy one when he is unsure who his client is.

In the competitive theatre world, it is hardly common for an actor on the rise to stand up to and tell off a valuable publicity source. That Karen would speak up didn't surprise me; that she spoke up for me did. I was and am grateful to her.

What bothered me was not What but Why. "Why" is always the question to be asked about anything. Why had Jesse Green whacked with such glee? Why had his editor ordered the whacking? Why did Michael Riedel do me in at every opportunity?

A simple answer was the Law of Theatre Gravity: What is up has to be brought down. Too simple, that answer, and not the whole answer *but the questions themselves were extraneous. What did the motives and practices of vultures matter anyway? I was ninety-two then; it was getting late to grow up.*

When I got home from wherever I was on the Friday of the week *New York* was on the newsstand, there were ominous messages from the press agent: the subject of Riedel's column the next day was going to be Matt Cavenaugh. It never rains. The considerate press agent wanted to give me a "heads up" on what was in the column. Whatever it was, I knew I would be shafted, so I didn't call. The next morning, one of the producers phoned to express sympathy because the column said I had fired Matt Cavenaugh. That producer knew even better than I that that was a lie.

Matt's performance, the performance that we had worked so hard to get, had only come together during the New York previews in time to garner the reviews he badly wanted. But that performance, he had stopped giving after three months. Instead, he reverted to being the standard musical comedy juvenile, too preppy for the streets of *West Side Story*. The show had become a well-paying job.

That broke the camel's back. For the two weeks he was away, his understudy, Matthew Hydzik, went on. He had gone on for Matt in Washington and had not been very impressive, but he had learned from watching what Matt did and didn't, and from the notes I gave Matt. When I rehearsed the second Matt before his first Broadway performance, he was not merely better than I expected but he opened up new windows for Tony, more sides to his character, more colors to his scenes. When Matt Hydzik went on, the whole show was better and fresher and the company was happier.

The producers had never been keen on Matt Cavenaugh; they had wanted him fired in Washington, but I had resisted. The show was coming up on playing a year—contract renewal time, and they didn't want to renew his contract to play Tony. This time, I didn't fight them. When the original Riff added abusing the girls he danced with in the execution of lifts to his whining complaints about everyone else, the producers paid him off and in came a new Riff—John Arthur Greene, who gave the Jets the leader they had always wanted and the show the jolt it needed. I wasn't about to fight producers like that for someone I had fought for too many times anyway and who was hurting the show.

All this began as an item in a gossip column—Michael Riedel's. His epitaph should be "Here Lies." His lie about the firing of Matt Cavenaugh was only one in a long list. Each made me the villain, no surprise, but each made the producers the heroes. That was a surprise, because Riedel's compliments are reserved for his clients.

There were similar surprises at the same time on the answering machine at home: "So how does it feel to know so many people hate you?" A year later: "Aren't you dead yet?"

Tom once found a box of human excrement on his doorstep. "It should have been wrapped in pretty paper and had a ribbon tied around it" was what he said. You can't wrap a ribbon around a phone message, but you can erase it. It's very easy, really.

Today, I don't give a thought to the trivia and the trivial mudslingers I never should have let get to me in the first place. Dealing with Tom's death, trying to come to terms with reality, whatever that reality is—it changes almost daily—everything else comes into perspective. Reputation is irrelevant to anything worth caring about.

I was discussing the *West Side Story* tour with Jim Youmans, who designed its stunning scenery as well as the equally stunning scenery for *Gypsy* and five of my plays. Jim is a joy to work with because he is not only a brilliant designer, he is the nicest man in the theatre. He was in the midst of a new Twyla Tharp adventure. How she was to work with?

"Tough," he said, "like you."

Like me? But it was Jim; my back didn't go up. "Exactly what does that mean?"

"You both know what you want, you demand it, you're determined to get it, and you do." He saw my face. He put an arm around me. "But you're very sweet," he laughed.

The Sunday morning before Christmas, I was snowbound by more than two feet of fresh snow outside the windows of my house in Quogue and watching the timeless Sophia Loren being interviewed on television.

The young interviewer, smiling, smitten but a bit nervous now, "I hope you don't mind if I bring up—well, everyone says your body, asks if your figure—"

The lady, lightly with a little smile: "It isn't true."

Interviewer: "But I haven't asked what—"

The lady, as before: "I know. I hear. It isn't true."

Interviewer, brightly, a bigger smile than ever: "Oh. Well. That settles that, I guess. The rumor is finished once and for all, here and now."

Sophia Loren: "No. They will keep saying it. It doesn't matter."

Fashion Plates: *Albert Wolsky and Theoni Aldredge were "not only perhaps the two best costume designers I know, but both dear friends."*

What doesn't matter is the subject of the title of this chapter. What does matter is what my friends think and how I continue to change as I try to live with loss. I think I have faced reality and accepted it: pain gone, tears gone, all quiet on the emotional front. Then I have dinner, as I did night before last, with Albert Wolsky, the Oscar-winning costume designer and an old friend grappling with the loss a year ago of his partner, James Mitchell, the actor/dancer who was an old, much-loved friend of mine. Advising Albert, consoling him. and oh, there it is, there I am, there's Tom, sitting on the edge of his hospital bed, swinging his legs, telling me to go home, he'll see me in the morning. Which never came, but the tears did, and they still well. What is reality now? That my state will always change. And that he will always be missed and that Quogue is home. That will never change.

FOUR

Friends

"Friend" is a small word with a large number of meanings. The range is from something more than acquaintance to something less than lover. Best friend, close friend, loving friend—none of those phrases is exactly right. One word, one umbrella word, for the someone who is special, whom you care deeply about, whom you completely trust and who has those same feelings for you—the last is essential: unless it's mutual, it isn't friendship. Just as love must be mutual to be love. But friendship is a kind of love, and a "friend" is a kind of lover.

Until I was seventeen, I never had a friend. Early on, at seven, I knew I was gay and allowed that to isolate me from the kids in the neighborhood and in school. There was a kid on the block who also was gay—you find each other—he and I had sex occasionally. He wasn't a friend, though. I didn't like him, but I liked sex, and there was no one else. At that time and place—Brooklyn in the thirties—sex of any kind wasn't mentioned until two good-looking English boys our age, early teens, arrived. With a lot of panache and chutzpah, they began reducing the number of virgins in the neighborhood. Female virgins.

MEMBER ASSOCIATED PRESS
FOUNDED 1880

𝔗𝔥𝔢 ℭ𝔬𝔯𝔫𝔢𝔩𝔩 𝔇𝔞𝔦𝔩𝔶 𝔖𝔲𝔫

INCORPORATED 1905

CORNELL UNIVERSITY
ITHACA, N.Y.

July 12, 1937

Dear Art:

      Enclosed you will find check
for $51.15 which is your share of the
profits of the Senior Week Issue of The
Sun.

      The issue was the biggest
ever put out, consequently the high
dividends.

      Don't spend this all in one
place and with best of luck to you.

Cordially,

Irv.

ht

A Working Writer: *The first of many paychecks Arthur would receive.*

When I went to London as an adult, I thought I must have gotten it wrong: those two boys could never have been English.

At seventeen, I became a junior counselor at a kids' summer camp and made friends with every boy my age or thereabouts rather desperately. I couldn't talk to them about anything I wanted to talk about—being homosexual, books, the theatre, politics. They talked about baseball and liked to play cards. I would say they were good All-American boys, except they were all Jewish.

In my senior year at college, I shared an off-campus apartment with another graduate of my summer camp. We talked like friends, acted like friends, but weren't friends. I did have two friends who were friends, though: Eve Merriam-to-be, my Ginger Rogers at proms, my name-changer when I went job hunting; and Paul Davison, the editor-in-chief of the *Cornell Daily Sun*. I was his assistant editor and best friend. Eve and I remained friends until she died. Paul and I lost each other when I went to visit him the year after graduation.

He was from Canandaigua in upstate New York; until he met me, he thought Jews had horns. He vouched for my sexuality, saying he personally could verify I wasn't queer because we had slept in the same bed and I hadn't touched him. He was six foot two, blond, handsome, reason enough to be vain, but I, not thinking it was, hadn't realized he was. Straight men are hung up about gay men: they automatically assume they're irresistible. Especially those who can't get a date. It was no effort not to touch Paul; I didn't find him attractive. I've never wanted a straight man, anyway.

Paul's girlfriend went to Ithaca College. She was the female version of him; they could have been a cereal poster. They did a lot of screwing in his car. In our senior year, after two abortions, she couldn't risk another. So they got married and lived bitterly ever after.

His dream had been to be a journalist; he would have made a very good editor, he was very talented. There was a newspaper job waiting, but it didn't pay enough to support a wife and a new baby. Insurance companies did; they moved to Hartford, the industry capital.

A bus took me from New York to see them. I walked into their apartment; directly in my line of vision was a shoebox divided into sections. Paul explained: one for rent money, one for food, for the baby, for utilities, for cigarettes, and for liquor. The apartment itself was small and grey; she was drunk; neither of them would have been chosen for a poster, and neither of them moved though the baby kept crying.

In Ithaca, we had great times; we laughed a lot. In Hartford, we sat and drank, all three of us wishing I hadn't come, all three of us sad we were no longer friends, all three of us glad I would never come back.

I had never had a friend like him. On the bus home, I doubted I would ever find another.

My roommate at Cornell followed in his father's Rotarian footsteps: he was a good husband, a good father, and he played golf. In college, he did crossword puzzles in ink. But there was a brighter side to him. We would count how many times he sneezed in a row—nineteen was his record. He had a parlor trick: he could throw his knee in and out at will with a little punctuating click. And, uncharacteristically, he quite enjoyed the car we co-owned—a bilious green wreck of a Buick with a big hole in the floorboard and brakes that kept locking. To unlock them, one of us had to piss on a wheel. While he preferred I make a fool of myself, he didn't balk when it was his turn. We got all along very well until two weeks before commencement.

The windows in the large bedroom we shared in our off-campus apartment opened directly on a veranda. The air was soft and balmy the night the president of our fraternity, a member of the baseball team and a ladies' man—he and I had occasionally double-dated, and then he and I had sex in the shower—crawled through the open window to my bed directly beneath it. For four years, he and I had sex—not an affair, sex. Always instigated by him, but he would never talk about it. It was as though we weren't actually doing anything.

The bedroom was pitch-black, but I knew my roommate was awake. I knew he couldn't tell exactly what we were doing, but could hear we were doing something. I knew that and went on deliberately. He revered the boy in bed with me. I thought that would help, knowing it wasn't just misfits like me. I wanted him to know; I wanted someone I could talk with, not just about the sex, about what I was, who I was. I wanted a friend.

In the morning, it was a Sunday, my roommate took the keys to our car and went out without a word. He didn't speak to me when he came back and only when absolutely necessary until the letter came. He left it open where he knew I had to see it. It was from another summer camper, older than either of us and in medical school. "X" was very sick and should see a psychiatrist immediately. It was the "X" that made me lose control. I was a thing doctors discussed! I accused, I shouted, he shouted back, we both shouted until we petered (sic) out. We were politely nice to one another for the rest of our time in the apartment. As though nothing had happened, the elephant was back on the coffee table. As it was with my real friend, my best friend, with Paul Davison, who didn't even know it was there. Why would he? He knew firsthand I wasn't queer.

When you're young, the need for a friend who will listen can be almost physically painful.

In wartime New York, in the midst of all that sex and booze, I made two friends who changed my life in very different ways: Jerome Robbins and Nora Kaye. The friendship with Jerry was fun and literally games until *West Side Story* opened in Washington to historic acclaim. That changed my life, but it also ended the friendship: my friend Jerry wanted all the acclaim to be his.

With Nora, it quickly became a love affair. We began talking marriage until she said she wouldn't care if I were unfaithful with a woman but would if I were with a man, because she couldn't compete with a man. I knew then that marriage would be unfair. I would be unfaithful with a man, it was inevitable, I would always want a man; I was not bisexual, whatever that was. To me, the ability to have and enjoy sex with a woman does not make a man who enjoys sex with men bisexual, let alone a man who prefers sex with men. The determining factor to me is emotional. The love I had for Nora or Anita Ellis or Lena Horne couldn't compare with the overwhelming love I felt for Tom Hatcher, a love I still feel. Sometimes I wish I didn't feel that love, life might be easier, but it was the best thing in my whole life. I have no choice.

Actually, I did. After living fifty-two years of the best years of my life, I had to confront living without him. The difficulty was in the small ways, such as not being able to begin the morning speaking with him. Even now, I inadvertently start, just for the briefest of moments, but I forget and begin. The killer difficulty, the difficulty I fear is permanent is how to live alone after sharing most of my life and assuming I always would. And if I wouldn't, that was decades away and Tom, being twelve years younger, would go first. That thought wasn't conscious, but the unconscious did well in our house.

Being alone was never a problem for me; I liked it, I welcomed it, but it was always by choice. It's by choice to an extent now: I would rather have dinner alone than with just anybody. Before, however, even though I may have been at the table alone, it was because he was there and I was here; it was momentary. Knowing that person is only temporarily not there is a fundamental security.

Nora and I remained friends for a long time. Shortly after she married Herb Ross, he needed a job. I was directing *I Can Get It for You Wholesale* for David Merrick and joked Merrick into hiring Herb and forgetting they were suing one another over an earlier show. After *Wholesale,* Herb directed as well as choreographed a musical called *Kelly.* It closed in one night. Nora didn't have to ask. I was directing *Anyone Can Whistle,* which I had written with Steve Sondheim, and brought in Herb to choreograph with Nora as his assistant. They did one of the wittiest comic ballets I have ever seen. Unfortunately, the show only ran nine performances, so the ballet wasn't seen by enough people to help Herb's career.

Nora was on to bigger game, anyway. Under her management, Herb ended up directing movies in Hollywood. When he was established, she called me: they wanted to do a movie about the ballet and I was the only one who could write a movie about the ballet.

I had stopped writing for the screen after an unhappy experience with *The Way We Were* five years earlier. Nora knew that. She also knew me and how much our friendship meant to me. The pot was sweetened with a promise I could coproduce to protect what I wrote. Hollywood was no mystery to me; I should have known it takes a good deal more than a title to protect a writer.

The Turning Point, as the ballet movie was called, originally had a prominent gay subplot that began to disappear, scene by excised scene. The conservative studio, I assumed. Herb had said I wasn't to worry about the studio. He was truthful about that. It was he who was cutting everything gay he could.

When I finally woke up, I was living with Nora and Herb in their house in Beverly Hills, which made confrontation a bit awkward. However, at the rate of castration, it was then or never. The showdown at the O.K. Corral took place in the lanai—porch in the East. Herb didn't deny cutting everything gay. Patiently, he explained that I didn't understand no one in the ballet was gay anymore.

I gaped at him; I looked at Nora. This was 1977, a year of no sexual upheavals I had heard about. The three of us had known one another for over thirty years; we knew everything sexual about one another. Herb had always been as gay as ten little red boots on the mantel. I didn't say that; I limited myself to categorizing sex as practiced in the ballet world and turned to Nora. She giggled. "It's like walking on eggs around here," she said, and duck-walked out of the lanai. Ballerinas walk like ducks; it's all those years in the fifth position.

Today, I would never have though of Herb Ross as a friend. He was loyal to no one; he had no notion what loyalty was. One—he—was either master or slave; people were either used or users. Whether or not he loved Nora I didn't know; I didn't know whether he was capable of love. I did know he was in awe of her, he worshipped her, she was his ultimate Yes or No.

Nora was a friend for a long time. Then the day came when she announced she wasn't. It wasn't when she threw in her towel as one of the artists in the ballet world of her time and became a Beverly Hills yenta; it was some time before that, the day Jerry Robbins was giving himself a birthday party. Do I have to invite Arthur, he asked Nora. "No," she said blithely.

It wasn't her answer that told me she was no longer my friend; it was

that she went out of her way to inform me of Jerry's question and her
answer. Nora behaved as a friend very much as she felt in the moment.
She saw neither inconsistency nor contradiction in this or any aspect of
her relationships. She once had both Jerry and me unknowingly preparing
to try marriage at the same time; instead she married Isaac Stern. A
honeymoon concert tour in South America and she divorced him. He was
too straight for her. Men who were primarily gay were attractive and
attracted to her. Herb Ross was the last of her experiments.

Herbie—I named the agent in *Gypsy* after him—was a great cook.
He, Nora, and I, their house guest, ate very well at their Beverly Hills
plantation during the shooting of *The Turning Point*. We also played
the game of Pals very well until Anne Bancroft spoiled it.

Annie and Tom and I had become good friends when she came
back to New York from California, where she had been Queen of
the B's. This was in the sixties, just before she dazzled the theatre
with her performances in *The Miracle Worker* and *Two for the Seesaw*,
two roles that couldn't have been more different. She was headed for
legend, but Annie wasn't driven and she was lazy.

On the set of *Turning Point*, she asked what I thought of a big
scene she had played the previous day.

"You did it with one hand behind your back," I said.

She knew exactly what I meant—there was little she didn't know
about acting—and said nothing. But I knew her and knew she was
pissed off. Very. She went to Herb and proclaimed I should be on the
set all the time with them or not at all.

Herb was patient with me once again. "You're not only a very
good writer, you're a very good director, so I think you should go
home."

Home I went.

Everything gay was eliminated from the picture except for a necessary plot point that seemed smuggled into the last scene.

The Turning Point received eleven nominations for the Oscar and won zero. I could say it ended my friendship with Nora—the friendship I cared about—but that isn't entirely true. She had changed. She had become a Beverly Hills matron in good standing and shopping. The powder room on the first polyurethaned floor was so completely covered in flowered wallpaper, you couldn't find the toilet. She and Herb-now-Herbert had matching Mercedes four-door sedans with his-and-hers license plates. There was a cutting room at the end of the manicured garden. She was asked to be artistic director of Ballet Theatre and refused.

It seems to be a rule that there's always an exception to the rule. Change, as in this instance, can be undesirable after all. The exception, however, is rare.

A Star Turn: *Arthur giving notes to his* Turning Point *star Anne Bancroft.*

When I left the country because I was blacklisted, I sailed for Paris on the Isle de France. I went tourist but spent most of the time in first class as the guest of Lena Horne and Lenny Hayton. We knew each other from open house at Gene Kelly's; we were friendly but not friends. By the time we docked at Le Havre, we were friends.

In Paris, Lena and I became more than friends. What we were, I don't quite know, but whatever it was, Paris was the perfect city to be it in. It was one of the happiest times of my life and hers. Whatever we were continued when we came back to the States but in a different form: we were loving friends and remained loving friends here and back in Paris, where she was singing and I was working on *Anastasia* with my friend Anatole Litvak, the director.

Paris is known as a city for women, which it made it perfect for Tola. He came from upper-class Russia; as a teenager, to escape the Russian Revolution, he hid in a brothel. The girls gave him an upbringing that made him love women. His first stop outside Russia was Paris; in Paris, he was home.

I used to work to keep the different worlds I lived in apart. That's the only explanation I can come up with for not introducing Lena and Tola. I loved both of them. I loved them even more after each met Tom and loved him. He and I hadn't been together very long when he came over to Paris to be with me. He had never heard Lena sing. When we went to hear her at the club where she was conquering Paris nightly, she was oddly nervous. She wanted to be good for Tom. She was magnificent. And of course, they became friends.

It's hazy, a blur—Lena and Paris, the times we were there together. She's in lilac and beige and we're walking under trees near the Ronde Point; we're drinking at the Mars Club, I get up to sing by the piano and she laughs gleefully; it's my birthday, which is Bastille Day, so all of Paris has joined her in celebrating with me; we're at a club in Miami where she had to enter by the back door; we're at the beach house in Quogue with Nora and Tom and she's making Sazeracs. I left Paris for the States, I'm all over the place, but that's what happens with remembering Lena: my mind is unable to settle, we were never able to settle. What made us unravel was *Hallelujah, Baby!*

It wasn't only that she had walked out on a musical I had written for her that no one else could do because it was so specifically for her; it was much more why she had walked out. She wrote me a remarkably honest letter of explanation, but I read it for me, not for her, not for what it cost her to write it, not for the love we had for each other that was all over it. I don't think how I read it would have changed the turn of events, but I wish I had. Rejection is never easy to take, but to be angry rather than understanding makes looking in the mirror very difficult. At least I can say I never showed the letter to anyone and threw it away so that no one else could ever read it.

What brought us back together was *Original Story By.* She read it and called me, called because she had been reminded of what she had forgotten: how happy she had been that time in Paris. When we talked after so many years, each of us was near tears. She wasn't too well, wasn't really going out. I called again, we talked, I called again and again but she wasn't going to let me see her.

In *Anyone Can Whistle*, the heroine says, "I'm glad I'm not a beauty because I never have to worry about being an ex-beauty." I don't know if that was the reason. At eighty, she was beautiful, I saw her on YouTube. Not beautiful in the way she had been in Paris, but beautiful, nothing had been done to her face, beautiful and serene.

Her knees were bad, and she didn't want to go through an

operation, but she wouldn't want me to see her on a walker, I thought. Then sometimes she wouldn't take the calls. Frustrated, I stopped calling.

Not too long ago, in Brighton, England, two new friends of mine showed one YouTube video after another of Lena singing songs I had never heard her sing, at various ages and stages. When I came home, I called her. She was not well, but I did make her laugh. That was one of those moments you want to put in a box and keep. I called again; same pattern but cut shorter. She wasn't seeing anyone but her daughter Gail, who kept looking more and more like her mother used to look; Lena wasn't talking to anyone but Gail.

Times changed, she changed, I changed, it's not a story with the happiest of endings. It's a love story, though, and love doesn't end. It fades but it stays here. I still imagine her in Paris; what we had, whatever it was, is still here.

Soon after *Gypsy*, Steve Sondheim cautioned that I went overboard with friendship, pointing out that I made a new friend one day, the next I was his or hers for life, and sooner or later I was disappointed. To me, it was better to risk being hurt than to close the door to someone who might be forever or close to it. That belief was modified by two gay men who taught me that a little restraint in the friendship department was advisable.

The pair of acolytes arrived on my scene in 1959. I know the year because of my custom of using the names of friends in the musicals I write. Nineteen-fifty-nine was the year of *Gypsy*, and besides Herbie were the names Zipser and Webber. In the first scene of *Gypsy*, Mr. Zipser is the drummer Rose asks to "ad lick it" for her girls; Mr. Webber, in the second scene, the man Rose asks to book her act in his vaudeville house. Zipser and Webber asked me to lend them the down payment on the land next to my beach house in Quogue.

I wouldn't hear of asking them to put anything in writing. My lawyer was aghast, but I got on a very high horse. They were friends; friends are trusted, friends do not have to sign anything.

Late that summer, the cleaning lady read in the *Hampton Chronicle* that the land my friends had bought with my loan had been sold. For a profit in which I didn't share. My loan wasn't returned, either. I got zip; Mr. Zipser and Mr. Webber skipped town and went to sunnier California. Mr. Webber, the younger and more attractive of the pair, got a job as secretary to the retired, quietly gay silent screen star Ramon Novarro. Novarro was murdered for money that wasn't in his house by the brother of a hustler he had long been friendly with. Out of a job and money, Webber and Zipser packed up and returned to New York in search of trusting new friends.

To celebrate my eightieth birthday, Tom threw a huge party in Quogue. I didn't know we had so many friends, and such notable ones. The highlight was the performance by Steve Sondheim and his young friend, Peter Jones—in a Merman wig and his own moustache—of an epic number Steve had written based on melodies from *Gypsy*. With Steve at the piano and P.J. doing most of the singing, they brought the house down with a hilarious and affectionate celebration of my career and birthday. Steve gave me a framed copy of the lyric, which hangs on a wall in my study at the beach. It has never been taken down, even in the stormiest times.

Thanks to Tom—who liked giving parties—the food was better than it usually is at those things, and AA or not, the drink was fine and plentiful. There was even a little welcome spice in the form of a flare-up between a woman who felt she had been outed in a book and the author who called her a lesbian in a louvered closet. No one

"Arthur's Turn": *On Arthur's eightieth birthday Stephen Sondheim wrote these new lyrics to the music of* Gypsy *(see pages 128—130), which were performed by "Merman" returned from beyond (Sondheim's then boyfriend Peter Jones).*

(To be sung by Ethel Merman, returning from the Great Beyond, with Ethel Merman inflections and panache)

THE ARTHUR LAURENTS 80TH BIRTHDAY SONG

(To the tune of the verse to "Everything's Coming Up Roses")

I had a show,
A wonderful show, Arthur,
A long time ago, Arthur.
And now, so I'm told,
You're eighty years old --
To me you're pure gold!
So, Arthur --

Here's a little medley of *your* favorites and mine.
          (To the pianist)
Mr. Zipser, hit it!

(To the tune of "Everything's Coming Up Roses")

You look swell, you look great,
Shit, you hardly look seventy-eight.
Starting here, from today,
Arthur, everything's coming up roses!

Clear the deck, clear the track,
You're the reason I had to come back.
Oh and hey, by the way,
Loads of love from Benay.
I'm here to see your wishes all come true!
Arthur,
Everything's coming up bigger and bigger hits,
Everything's coming up cheering and heavy mitts,
Everything's coming up ski trips to St. Moritz ...

And speaking of hits, Arthur, did I ever tell you about me and Jerry Orbach in the revival of *Annie*? One night I caught him making faces during my big speech in the boat scene. And you know what I did? I marched right up to him after the show and I said, "Listen, Jerry," I said, "What are all those faces you're making during my big speech in the boat scene?" And he said, "Why, Ethel, I'm just reacting to what you're saying." And I said, "Look, Jerry, I don't react to your lines, you don't react to mine! Okay?" You see, I'm like you, Arthur I never let reactions get in my way. It takes more than reactions to stop old pros like us from what we're doing!

(To the tune of the release of "Small World")

We have so much in common,
It's a phenomenon.
I think of us as equal,
Let's do a sequel ...

But that wouldn't be your style, would it, Arthur? Because you never repeat yourself! Like some others I could mention. And will.
          (To the pianist)
Hit it!

(To the tune of "Some Prople")

Some playwrights get lots of praise
Just rewriting their early plays --
That's okay for some playwrights
Who don't know that they're hacks.

Some playwrights get panned a lot,
Grow too bitter and go to pot.
That's perfect for some playwrights
Who stop dead in their tracks.

But you,
You always come through
With something that's
Both tradition and innovation:
Cuckoo, Clearing, Home Of The Brave,
Enclave, Bird Cage, Invitation
Each one gets my personal rave!

And I woulda seen 'em, too, if I hadn't been workin' at the time!

Some playwrights can be content,
Making pageants or faking *Rent.*
That's peachy for some playwrights
For some numb dumb playwrights, and their shows.
Well, they can stay and rot
Or write prose!

Okay, so I didn't see the plays, but I saw the movies. And Arthur,
I gotta tell ya, they were great! But as my old friend Cole Porter
said, Let's Face It -- why didn't you think of me for some of those
roles? With what I got inside of me -- if I ever let it out --
Anastasia -- *there* was a part I coulda sunk my teeth into! And what
about *Snake Pit? Bonjour Tristesse? Rope?* You coulda *written* them
for me. For me! For me! For me! Still ...

(To the tune of the verse to "Everything's Coming Up Roses")

We did a show!
You wrote it for me, Arthur!
It fit to a "t", Arthur!
But you gotta agree:
If it wasn't for me,
Where the hell would you be?

I made Porter, I made Gershwin, I made Berlin and I made you! And I
can do it again! I will, Arthur, I swear I will! I'm gonna make *you* a
star! You're gonna write a whole new show all about me! It's gonna
be better than anything you ever did before! Better than anything
you even dreamed! Finished? Why, you're just beginning, and there's
no stopping you this time!

3.

(To the tune of "Have an Eggroll, Mr. Goldstone")

Happy birthday, Mr. Laurents!
Have a vodka, have a sand dune, have a smash!
Have a memoir, Mr. Laurents --
It'll be a catharsis as well as a source of cash.

Have a drink, have a snort,
Read a book, watch the court,
Deal the cards out, overbid.
Take a bath, take a nap,
Just don't take any crap --
But of course you never did!

Happy birthday, Arthur Laurents!
Feel the love, the admiration -- can you feel?
Though the fondness all around you
May astound you,
It's real!
How have you survived the biz,
Full of fight and full of fizz?
Kid, you must be made of steel.

The producers, the actors,
The myriad factors
That make the the-ay-ter insane,
All the Clurmans, the Hermans --
No, there's only one Merman --
Have we heard you complain?
Ho-ho!
Ha-ha!

Happy birthday, Arthur Laurents,
May our wishes for your happiness come true.
Our affection comes in torrents
And it warrants
This do.
Sartre but with sex appeal,
The funniest playwright since O'Neill,
Arthur Laurents, we love you!

Happy birthday!

                                        July 14, 1997

"No Fits, No Fights, No Feuds and No Egos, Amigos": *The "adorable"*
Jule Styne and his "delicious" wife, Margaret.

really cared one way or the other, but they gave the party the kick every good party needs.

A bit of the bloom was off the rose for me because of who hadn't come and why. That couldn't happen today; I've changed, and who showed, who didn't, wouldn't matter. But today, I wouldn't give a party like that.

We used to give a notable New Year's Eve party. It began with a black-tie dinner for eight, then the door opened for friends and a few they asked to bring. What made it special wasn't the famous faces—except the year of Vivien Leigh—it was that New Year's Eve was Jule Styne's birthday: the champagne toast at midnight was first to him, then to the new year. A party for a friend has a warmth and an intimacy a party to celebrate an event doesn't. When Jule died, the party died with him. We stopped giving it.

When Tom was seventy, he announced he wasn't going to do anything he didn't want to from then on. Prominent on his list was spending time with friends who weren't worth it. Most of the friends he meant were in AA—he referred to everyone in AA as a friend. One or two members of his home AA group were friends or came close enough. Since he was by nature a caretaker, there were too many others constantly at his door. Eliminating them gave us so much more time together, I didn't hesitate to encourage the wholesale dumping of those who didn't make the cut.

My equivalent of AA is the theatre. After all these years, there are several whom I more than like, but "friends"? One of my oldest friends is not in the theatre; he's never been part of my public life. That's why he isn't in either of my other books and why I wanted to write about him in this. It's also why he said a vehement "No, thank you" to the use of his name, to any allusion to his existence that might lead a journalist or researcher to come looking for him—because of my notoriety, which is much less than he thinks—and ask questions about him, me, us, sometime in the future. The implication is the questions will be asked after I'm gone.

That didn't offend me. He doesn't like to talk about death any more than most people do, but we are all going to die, and that's when academics and vultures do come a-hunting and asking. What it did do, though, was make me remember that before Tom died, I blithely said I was never going to die. What's more, I believed it. Two specific times after he died, I wished I were dead. Then I accepted I was going to die like everyone else. Now the circle is complete: I'm back to believing I'm never going to die. That doesn't have to be a fantasy. I've always taken a nap in the afternoon. If, one time, I didn't wake up, I'd never know I hadn't lived forever.

Stephen Sondheim was my first friend in the theatre. The year was—well, we met in New York after *The Time of the Cuckoo* opened but before Tom came to live with me, which means it was either late in 1953 or sometime in 1954. Whenever it was, I was considering writing a musical based on James M. Cain's *Serenade,* a novel about a gay opera singer who suddenly loses his voice. The enthusiastic producer brought Steve to play some of the score for his first as yet unproduced musical, *Saturday Night. Serenade* went nowhere, because work on *West Side Story* started. The rest is theatre history: a lyricist was needed to collaborate with Lenny Bernstein, Steve's lyrics had impressed me, the trio of collaborators became a quartet.

While working on *West Side,* Steve and I began a friendship that lasted fifteen rollicking years. What we shared was a love of the theatre, all kinds of theatre, not just the musical, though that dominated. We had very dissimilar backgrounds. I came from

"From Your First Cigarette to Your Last Dying Day":
Steven Sondheim and Arthur Laurents.

Friends Indeed: *Angela Lansbury, Arthur Laurents, and Steve Sondheim at the AIDS Benefit concert of* Anyone Can Whistle.

middle-class Brooklyn and lived happily with a male lover. Steve lived alone, was alone but very much at home in the Bucks County houses of the upper-crust theatre world, where Oscar Hammerstein had begun mentoring him when he was a precocious teenager. Even though I'd had a success on Broadway, I was on the periphery of that world, just as I'd been on the periphery of the Beverly Hills movie world even though I'd written a Hitchcock movie. Was the reason the same as the reason I had no friends in my childhood—that I was gay—or was it because I never wanted to belong to any world except that of the village of Quogue? The answer wouldn't matter except that it hangs it whether or not the choice was mine.

My friendship with Steve hit its peak while we were writing *Gypsy*. Every moment of the collaboration was enjoyable, every moment of

"Hey Old Friend": *Arthur Laurents and Steve Sondheim in the living room at St. Lukes.*

our friendship was enjoyable, Jule Styne was enjoyable, and that's the entire cast. Jerry Robbins, who was going to choreograph and direct, was busy with the London production of *West Side Story*, and David Merrick, the chief producer, was busy making mischief with another of his shows. It was just the three of us, a reason I think *Gypsy* turned out so well. And because it was going so well is another reason Steve and I were doing so well as friends.

Next came *Anyone Can Whistle*, which didn't do so well, and neither did we. Then came *Do I Hear a Waltz?*, which did even worse and was a dreadful experience, particularly for Steve. Richard Rodgers, who was the composer and the producer, was a lesson: never have a creative collaborator as the producer. His treatment of Steve was appalling at best.

Poems from the Maestro: Faded signature reads, "With undying affection over the years, Lenny" dated 1982 for Arthur's sixty-fifth birthday; and a poem titled "Insomniad," May 8, 1980.

The company was gathered on stage in Boston to rehearse a new lyric Steve had written when a flush-faced Richard Rodgers held up his hand for attention. Waving the copy of the new lyric Steve had handed him, he shouted at Steve, "Do you expect me to ask my company to sing this shit?" Steve went white, said nothing, and walked off the stage, down the aisle, and out of the theatre.

He had been a teenager mentee of Oscar Hammerstein of Rodgers and Hammerstein when Dick was the Royal Composer of Broadway. Now Oscar was gone, leaving Dick, a bad alcoholic, at a loss and losing ground every minute, while Stephen Sondheim was a bright star on the horizon. That may make Dick's behavior understandable, but it doesn't make it excusable. It was godawful for everyone on that stage then. Now it just seems like a sad anecdote.

Steve hadn't wanted to do *Do I Hear a Waltz?*. It came from *The Time of the Cuckoo*, which he said didn't sing. He also said he'd only done *Waltz* because I had pressured him and he was afraid of losing my friendship. That was said to Tom later, not to me. He wasn't right, he wouldn't have lost my friendship, but he pre-empted that issue. I did pressure him; I thought *Cuckoo* would make a lovely, small musical. It didn't.

Steve and I seemed to have recovered soon after *Waltz* opened: on the phone daily, dinners, theatre, weekends in Quogue. He talked more to Tom than to me, but he always had. Then he asked me to lunch at the Russian Tea Room. There was no leading up, no chit-chat, no warning; if there had been, the shock might have been less. But, well rehearsed, he went right into it: I was too strong an influence and he had to stop seeing me, our friendship was kaput. Pretty much just like that.

I hadn't seen it coming. I loved him, I loved us. I was devastated and I was hurt. Hurt lingers. Like cancer, it can go into remission but it keeps coming back. In recompense, or so I thought, he engineered a London production of *Gypsy* to be directed by me. One drunken night during previews, we wound up in a taxi with love in free fall in the back seat. One moment, then it was back to hurt.

It was exacerbated at times by something he might say about whatever I was directing or by a note he might write—one letter was so cruel, I wasn't able to read all of it the first time around—but hurt and rejection can breed childish payback. I took swipes at him in my books that I should not have. Lingering hurt is no excuse.

It no longer lingers. I've changed, he's changed, our relationship has changed. It's not a friendship anymore; we're not friends by any definition. But we're amicable, amiable; occasionally we use our old shorthand. Where we are with one another is a good place. It's easier for me, and it probably is for him. Anything that makes life easier for two people is good.

My closest friend is David Saint. We met in 1991 at the Seattle Repertory Theatre. He was associate director and I was doing a workshop of a new play, *My Good Name*. Neither of us was too happy when we ran into each other on a street by the theatre; we talked and kept talking. The following summer, he directed *My Good Name* at the Bay Street Theatre.

Tom met David and, seeing how much I liked him, said, "He's a boy, we have to make a man of him." So we set to work to bring him up, and our boy became a wonderful man. By that time, he was artistic director of the George Street Playhouse in New Brunswick and I was doing more plays with him—he usually directed but sometimes I did—than I had ever done with anyone, and we were friends, loving friends, the best of friends. Not because of all the

THE STAR LEDGER

Director/Writer: *Arthur told me, "Look serious, like we mean business" for this photo.*

theatre; theatre was our day job. It was because we had so much in common all over the human map and complete trust in one another.

The night that woman at Sloan-Kettering called to say Tom was dead, I called David and said, "Tom's dead." My voice was dead,

David tells me. He had taken something to make him sleep; he couldn't drive, so he called Stephanie, a girl at the George Street Playhouse who is an emotional emergency room. She drove David to Sloan-Kettering. We had already gone, Tom had already been taken away, but he found Tom's nurse, who described Tom's last minutes.

He was sitting up in his bed, the smile and twinkle intact as he chatted with the nurse. How was she feeling, how was her family, did she like nursing, did she like Sloan-Kettering, and a gusher of blood poured out of his mouth and he was dead.

David called the house on St. Luke's Place. We were still up. Stephanie drove him there, then left him there to take care of me because I was lost, gone somewhere no one knew. He put me to bed and for two weeks made sure I ate while he answered the phone and kept the house running. When I came back into the present wanting to go to Tom's park, he made sure I was taken there. I walked into the park, burst into tears, and you know what followed.

When you suffer the enormity of a loss as I did, that's when for the first time you understand the value of a friend, that's when you need friends. It's not easy for them, because you probably look as though you know what's going on but you really don't, and you keep changing and changing for a long time, more than three years in my case, and I think I may be changing again. Friends who love you are irreplaceable, but no one is as helpful as someone else who has had a similar loss. For me, it was Bernadette Peters.

We had been friendly, but now she became my friend. People who suffer loss find each other and reach out to each other. It's like one of those sermons except that it's true and the sole purpose is to help, not to convert or collect. Bernadette's husband, Michael, had been killed in a helicopter accident abroad about a year before Tom died. She was a year ahead of me; thus she knew the whereabouts of my pain and my grieving and my belief that Tom was here, that I could talk to him, that there were no coincidences and –that items like the *West Side Story* script in Spanish with corrections in his handwriting were signs from him. We sat across from each other at tables, we talked on the phone or in intermissions about death. It helped so much; it helped me, it helped both of us. It kept bringing us closer and closer until a deceptive occurrence threatened to change everything and throw us out of whack.

I wrote a play called *Come Back, Come Back, Wherever You Are,* largely to find out how I was dealing with loss. One of the two leading roles was for Bernadette; I would direct—we had long wanted to do something together—and it would be done at the George Street Playhouse, which would be a boon for David Saint. Bernadette Peters in New Jersey and in a role where she sang two songs? Sold out before it opened.

Bernadette had been encouraging while I wrote, keeping up to date on where I was and how I felt. When the play was finished, I sent it to her. She loved it: it was a beautiful play, her role was beautiful, but.

But? She couldn't do it. Why not? It was so close to her emotionally, to play it would be too painful.

My reaction was predictable when it shouldn't have been. Bernadette was my friend; that was not to be forgotten, but it was. In my defense, such as it is, I had planned this too carefully, I had banked on it too much. I sent her an eloquently persuasive e-mail; David said, "If this doesn't get her, nothing will." It didn't and nothing could have. While I was writing the play, she knew it would be too painful for her to do it but didn't tell me because she feared it might

Dashing Couple: *Bernadette Peters and Arthur
at a George Street Playhouse gala.*

stop me writing. I forced myself to accept that, behaved moderately well, but remained at a remove.

Bernadette came to the opening with a girlfriend. We had dinner before with David and some members of his board. She was Bernadette. At Tom's memorial in his park, she was one of three well-known actresses, but she was the one people gravitated to because she was herself, a person, not an actress. Her shoes were off. At that dinner, she wasn't the Broadway star, she was a friend, available to everyone but scarcely able to contain her excitement, her eagerness to see the play which, by then, I was feeling very good about.

Bernadette was awash at the end. She loved the play even more than when she'd read it; it was even more beautiful in performance than it had been on the page. And she was more convinced than ever that she couldn't do it, not ever, it would be too painful, it would always be too painful.

And then I got it; finally, I got it. It was so simple. Bernadette said what she meant. What she said was completely understandable. Some part of me, some lucky or changed part of me held on to my friendship with her and prevented me from throwing it away. I had changed while I was asleep at the switch. I learned. When you've had a loss bigger than life and you're trying to work out being alone in life—friends. Friends will be there to listen, to take, to give, to everything that will bring you back to life.

Tom never told me he was going to die. The only person he did tell was our friend who rented the one other house besides Tom's on the north perimeter of the park, and he asked him for help.

Alan Best, a short seller with ethics—difficult to believe but true—has changed markedly since he and his wife, Shelley, moved in. Shelley is an original, lovely, pretty, but always an original. It only seems that they've been renting that house since it was built; I can't visualize it without them in it any more than I can visualize our life in Quogue before or my life in Quogue now without them a large part of it. Alan has changed more, but Shelley's changed a lot, both largely because of Tom, partly because of the effect Tom's relationship with me had on them. They wanted to have what we had—whatever it was they saw. I don't know exactly what they or others like them saw. Perhaps that we liked each other and were happy together, unlike couples in the world of Dow Jones. Well, unlike most couples, period. That seems to be truer now than ever—the disturbing disintegration of the country seeping into the bedroom, I would guess.

When Tom told Alan he was going to die, he asked him not to tell anyone else, no one, not his wife and, underlined, not me. Vehemently, not me. He was doing everything possible to make life

Good Neighbors: *Tom with beloved next-door neighbors Alan and Shelley Best.*

after his death as easy as possible for me and for his brother. All business had already been transferred to our accountants. Not knowing his real purpose, I had driven him over so he could hand them his computer—he did all the banking and bill paying online. His explanation was that the transfer was to protect his strength from being sapped while he was undergoing chemo. I believed him. I always believed him. I believed him even when he wasn't here. The latter has changed; I don't do that anymore because I can't, not because I don't want to.

The night Tom died, an unpleasantness in the hospital would have gotten ugly if Alan hadn't been there. Hospital questions were being asked that I couldn't hear, let alone deal with. Alan took over quietly, I waited for I didn't know what. Then I did hear the voice with the clipboard mention disposal of the body. Tom's will clearly stated that he was to be cremated, his ashes to be buried in his park.

His brother objected almost violently: the ashes were to be buried in the Presbyterian cemetery next to those of their parents.

All the anger and rage in me that Tom was dead erupted like hot lava. He had left the Presbyterian Church because the minister preached homosexuality was a sin, he wanted to be buried in the park, he was going to be buried where he wanted—Alan stepped in. He knew all about Solomon: there would be two urns. And there are. One is buried to the left of the bench we always used to sit on and have our talks; mine will be buried to the right.

To anyone who hasn't yet acknowledged mortality, that notion may seem sentimental. To anyone who has suffered loss, nothing is sentimental, everything is mortal, nothing may happen after death, but what happens to what's left of us has to be given consideration. Tom and I had to be buried as we planned—alongside each other. Knowing that we would be is a comfort. Small, but a comfort where there was none.

And then, something I never imagined: an actual advantage to having suffered a loss.

In *Original Story By*, there is a photograph of my oldest friend in the world, a world very different from the one in which we met. That was, good Lord, more than sixty-five years ago, shortly before the Hollywood Witch Hunt we weathered together. Her name is Lorry Kaufman; in the photograph, she's smiling as she leans against the railing of her house in the Hollywood hills, very pregnant with my goddaughter Mary. She still lives in Los Angeles; everything I loved about her is intact, she hasn't changed. That amazes me. I'm amazed anyone even survives that town—but then, it isn't the company town it was, nor is it the glamorous trap it was.

Lorraine Kaufman was the first female psychiatric anthropologist.

That may sound intimidating, but she wasn't and isn't. She's too lovely, too gentle, everything about her is gentle except her giggle, which is like a waterfall. When we met, she was going to Judd Marmor as I was, working in locked wards as I wasn't—she was an admittedly forbidding combination of anthropologist and psychiatrist, but she settled down to being a therapist. Therapists can't even intimidate their own patients.

The work wasn't enough for her; she wanted to let out what that gentleness was covering. At eighty, with no training whatsoever, she began painting between patients. Watercolors of invented flowers that were more than just pretty; then, without warning, the watercolors were gone; she was using acrylic to paint fantasy blue horses on a carousel, then blue horses flying, then wild, aggressive blue horses on wood, most recently, a blue horse with a human heart. If you keep going, age doesn't matter; it can actually free you because what the hell, you're loving what you're doing, which is why you're doing it. Yes, that old maxim, but some of them are true.

She married Millard Kaufman before he became a Marine in World War II, which was long before he created the character of Quincy Magoo for movie cartoons and even longer before he wrote the screenplay for *Bad Day at Black Rock*. They were together longer than Tom and I, longer than any couple of any sex I've ever known. Then Millard wrote his first novel and finally died. I say "finally" because she worked so hard to keep him alive for so long. When he did die, what she needed was someone to talk to who knew about loss. I was her best friend and for the first and probably last time, I was glad I knew because I was able to help her the way Bernadette Peters had helped me. I was ahead of Lorry the way Bernadette had been ahead of me. I still am, and she still needs the help. It comes long distance and through letters. Yes, in the twenty-first century, letters: hers handwritten, mine typed on the computer. My handwriting went to hell in a handbasket a long time ago. She has always written in a lovely hand letters that resemble little essays; I collect them. Since Millard died, they are much less opaque, much more emotional, much more revealing. I answer with a letter until one sentence will tell me she needs more; I phone immediately. She's beginning to recover, beginning to change. I hope she is much better by November, when I will see her in Los Angeles.

I loathe Los Angeles. We last met there in 2000; I was on a brief book tour, flogging *Original Story By*. I hadn't been back since *The Turning Point* and its subsidiary obligations—attending the Golden Globes and the Oscars. The city was unrecognizable: space and air were gone, the drive-ins were gone, threatening high rises narrowed the boulevards; it was the ugliest city I'd ever been in. I was never going back. But I am, in November. Because the national tour of the production I directed of *West Side Story* will be playing there. I needed an excuse, I think, for not going before to see Lorry.

I'm a little afraid of that meeting. We won't have seen each other for a dozen years. Twelve years barely make a noticeable difference when you're forty or fifty or even sixty. When you get to be seventy, no matter what you've done to your face, it's changed, you no longer look like yourself. Lorry and I are both a lot more than seventy; surely we've changed, surely we don't look like we did.

I once started to write a sequel to *The Way We Were*. Early on, there would be a phone call between Katie Morosky (Barbra Streisand) in California and Hubbell Gardner (Robert Redford) in New York. On the phone, they would look as they were when photographed, but what he would see in his mind would be Streisand as Katie, across the street from the Plaza Hotel in the last scene of the original film, and what she would see would be Redford, the very blond lieutenant in his white uniform asleep at the Stork Club bar in the original. Two different people. The discrepancy when they finally met up again would be a huge obstacle to renewing a romance in which beauty was so important. That killed that idea for a sequel.

Thinking about the discrepancy after many years and meeting with Lorry in November, I looked at pictures of Tom in our first years and Tom in his last two years. He's changed a great deal; I don't know if a stranger would know it's the same person. I do, of course. His head has the same shape; his mouth and nose haven't changed, but it's the smile and the twinkle that do it. They're still there; it's Tom. I think he was better looking when he got older.

In November, unlike Tom, Lorry and I won't look better. Not a prayer, but it won't matter. We will be moved at just being together again after all this time. The letters tightened our bond.

There's another photograph of a very old friend in *Original Story By*. This one is of Millie Rowland, regally beautiful, sitting with her elegant husband Toby standing as her consort. The caption says they were celebrating their fiftieth wedding anniversary but doesn't say the high-style pose is because the photograph was taken by no less than Tony Armstrong, Lord Snowdon, husband of Princess Margaret, their friend. And a talented mimic. Decades ago, five of us were smoking grass in the Hamptons when he picked up a pornographic novel and began reading aloud with the unmistakable non-lilt in the voice of the Queen of England. It would have been very funny anyway, but the fact that the Queen was his mother-in-law made it hilarious. Pedigree is not for naught; neither is pot.

Both Millie, who was born in Seattle, and Toby, who was born

English Roses: *Millie Rowland with Arthur in her garden*
in Brighton, his last visit, the summer before his death.

in Montana, were English citizens by the time that photograph was
taken. Millie is ninety-three now and lives in Brighton, England.
What is extraordinary is that at ninety-three, it's all usually pretty
much settled: you are what you are and your life is what it is. Not so
with Millie. At ninety-three, she has a completely new life, better
than any she ever had; she is happier than she has ever been, all
because she is loved as she had never been by two gay men. She

came to Quogue once again last summer, bringing the boys, as she called them, exulting in the new life they had given her and in what they had done for me. They had given me a second shot at life.

There's a picture—everyone takes pictures with their cell phone these days but me—a picture of the four of us on the steps going down to the beach. It's a misty day and both boys are forty-seven, but the four of us look like something from an Abercrombie catalogue. Amazing what love can do.

I met Millie shortly after Tom arrived in New York; she was a quasi assistant to my soon to be ex-business manager—a man with a poodle. She became part of our life and remained there, even after she moved to London. Tom and Millie were probably closer than she and I were. She told him things she never told me. Par for our course. She crocheted him a needlepoint sampler of AA's Serenity Prayer in Spanish, which hangs on the wall outside his bedroom in his house in Quogue.

During the last years of Toby's life—he, too, died of cancer—and the many years after, our visits to London were brightened by dinner and theatre with Millie. No matter how we tried to arrive first, she was at the restaurant table reading when we got there. But I read my new plays to her in the sitting room of her house in Smith Street, off the King's Road.

She was almost too happy to see us, almost dancing down the street to welcome us. There was a lesson from the visit where she stopped dancing and seemed to have given up on life. We didn't know why. Whatever it was gave the evidently inevitable future a grim look. Two visits later, however, she was more alive than before and dancing faster. How come? What had made the change?

Her knees had quit on her. Millie Rowland would never, will

never complain about anything, least of all anything physical. She had resigned herself to seeing herself out, sitting in her sitting room at Smith Street. But the life force was too strong in her. She had both knees operated on at once—she was in her eighties—and came roaring back to life.

The relationship between physical and emotional well-being is the subject of too many TV programs to be news, but that doesn't make it any less important. Having re-launched herself, Millie then became a Millie I had never seen before.

She came over for the Broadway opening of the *Gypsy* I directed with Patti LuPone because Tom had urged me to, and brought Simon with her. She had been touting Simon; I had to meet Simon. Neither she nor I knew it, but I had met Simon almost ten years earlier: he's the "respected young agent" I mention in Chapter Two.

Simon Beresford was one of the two boys; the other was Keith Honhold-Beresford. They had been together for twenty years and married for five. It was a shock to realize England was that far ahead of us with same-sex marriage. My England went back to an after-theatre supper with John Gielgud at which he told me all the details of his arrest for soliciting in a public tearoom (toilet) and how Dame Sybil Thorndike had saved his career by coming on stage on his arm for his first entrance after his very public appearance in court.

I had just met Gielgud that evening. He was almost a child, he was so open, one of the reasons everyone adored him. Well, not Olivier, but that was for business reasons as well as vanity.

Keith is no longer in the theatre; he does events. They have long lived in Brighton and got Millie to live there—with a little push from me without knowing what Brighton was. The boys lived there, that was enough for me. Now that I have been to Brighton, I know why it is the place for Millie and Simon and Keith to live and for me to visit.

Brighton is a pretty seaside resort town that is more than twenty-five percent gay, which has had a salutary effect. People of all sexes walk hand in hand, everyone says "Hello," everyone is friendly; it's like the Village used to be before AIDS. I don't know the connection between gay and friendly, but there is one; someone writing a thesis might get a grant to find out what is.

I have never liked staying in anyone else's house, so I would never travel to go there. In all the years of my friendship with Steve Sondheim, I went to his house in Connecticut exactly once: Tom was in South America and I was out of excuses. These days, I am eager to go to Brighton, where Millie has a room just for me in her lovely, high-ceilinged flat. The flat is in one of those freshly painted white Victorian houses that decorate the cities of England. Millie's is across the road from a gated, private garden; beyond the garden is the beach, beyond the beach is the ocean, beyond the ocean's horizon is Quogue. I don't do any work while I'm there, I don't even think of doing any, and I'm completely taken care of. The food is great—both the boys cook—I sleep a lot, I walk in the garden across the road, I go up to London to see a few plays with Simon, I have a long, three hours or so, drink with Larry Dalzell, Simon's former boss. Larry knows more about the theatre than anyone I know, including David Saint and me.

Millie and I watch tennis; I'm in Brighton for Wimbledon. We don't go to Wimbledon. Why would we? Simon and Keith can project TV or movies on a huge wall in their living-dining room. For us, better than watching from less than great seats and worrying about the weather and food. We're not the rabid fans we were, but we're rabid about Rafa Nadal, wish Marat Safin hadn't partied so much, and dislike Andre Agassi for his snotty putdown of Pete Sampras in his tell-all book.

The time in Brighton goes as it always does when you're content: too fast.

It's impossible for Keith to be still; he has to be doing something for someone, always for Millie. He is a caretaker, which is why he reminds me constantly of Tom. Both of them, Simon as well as Keith, take care of Millie, of Larry, of me—I have never met anyone as generous, as giving as they are. And they enjoy it; they literally don't understand why I make such a big deal of it. It gives *them* pleasure.

In a short time, Simon became an English version of David Saint in so many ways. When writing a new play, I would read each new scene to Tom; I depended on his reaction and comments. I will always miss them, but I knew, after he was gone and I had finally started a new play, I needed someone to show it to as I wrote. David Saint was a natural someone, I began getting his help; now I get Simon's help as well and am doubly blessed. Each is different, each is invaluable, each is responsible for a change in me and my life.

Last summer, when Brighton came to Quogue, Tom's house was happy again. There was one evening of champagne and oysters with Alan and Shelley when we were all as delirious as we often had been in the days of Tom. All because of Millie and two new friends. In the midst of so much joy, I realized what I shouldn't have had to realize, that the best friend I ever had in my life was Tom.

Last night, I was reading a novel called *Let the Great World Spin* by Colum McCann, and I came to a chapter in which a woman is recalling the last day she spent with her dead lover. The love was

The Boys of Brighton: *Simon Beresford and his partner,*
Keith Honhold–Beresford, with Arthur.

in little details, each so poignant that identification brought out emotion I thought I had packed up and safely assigned to cold storage. I had to stop reading. Earlier today, I went back to the book.

The lover, a priest of sorts, was in a hospital, dying because of a car crash. The woman wanted to know where he was at the end, what he was thinking, what he was feeling; she wanted so much for him and also for herself. And then I came across this sentence:

"I can only hope that in the last minute he was at peace."

At that moment, I saw Tom in his blue hospital gown, sitting on the edge of his bed, saying calmly, "I want you to know I'm at peace." Not being religious, I didn't fully understand what he was saying. Now, because of this book, I do. I know he was happy at the end, and that makes me happier than I have been since he left.

Writing can make the amorphous concrete; writing can change the perception of pain from loss; writing this chapter was a catharsis just as writing a play about loss, *Come Back, Come Back, Wherever You Are*, was a catharsis. No matter how many times the pain from the loss of Tom changed, no matter how much the intensity decreased, it was always there, gnawing away, until this was written. Now the pain has gone. It was so familiar, evidence he was still here, that I almost miss it. Almost, but not quite. I never know precisely how I am going to feel about his absence. The other day, having lunch with his brother David, I was suddenly angry that Tom had left me. That was a new one.

There will never be anyone like him in my life; I know that as I've always known it. Nor do I want anyone in my life as a lover of any kind. I never wanted less in any area of my life, and I particularly don't in this one because I had so much. Besides, I'm too old. Never mind all the complimentary remarks on my appearance and creative energy and plain physical energy, etc.—they're encouraging and I'm grateful but not deceived. Old is old, and only an old fool doesn't know it.

When I awoke this morning, I felt like something washed up on the beach in front of my house. Writing this book, this chapter, drained everything out of me. Writing a play, even *Come Back, Come Back, Wherever You Are,* a play about Tom, didn't do anything like this to me. It was fiction; fiction is safe; it doesn't make you dig ever deeper, down to emotional depths you almost drown in. Yet there's a relief in getting down there, in getting all of it out. It frees me. I don't have to write about him or talk about him to keep him alive. He lives in me and in the friends who love him, and that has to be enough even though it isn't. It never will be.

FIVE

Catching Up

*L*iving life alone is difficult for me. I was questioning whether I had a future worth staying around for when I got an idea for a play I knew I had to write, a play I should have written years ago. It's about a middle-class Jewish family that discovers its adored son is gay. It takes place in the fifties, which, of course, is when it happened. It's written, much funnier than I thought it would be, but the surprise is always devoutly to be hoped for.

Now back to how I originally started this last chapter.

What is historical fact? What makes it fact? Being recorded? Written down on stone, papyrus, a hard drive? Has there ever been a completely objective writer? Is his word, spread by believers, fact because it's fact to them? Is the Bible fact? Is Jesus a fact? Which Jesus? Is the Koran fact? Is Buddha fact? What is fact? Is there historical fact?

These questions from the stratosphere came down to earth as I read what I had written about *West Side Story* in *Mainly on Directing*. It was closer to a press release than historical record.

The show was only two weeks into its Washington tryout in

December of 2008, but something had to be written because of the whole title: *Mainly on Directing: "Gypsy," "West Side Story," and Other Musicals.* The "something" had to be positive, of course; the production had cost fourteen million dollars that had to be recouped and turned into a profit somehow. I focused on the Spanish.

That had been enthusiastically welcomed when it was announced, but in the nation's capital, it got hate mail: "This is America! We

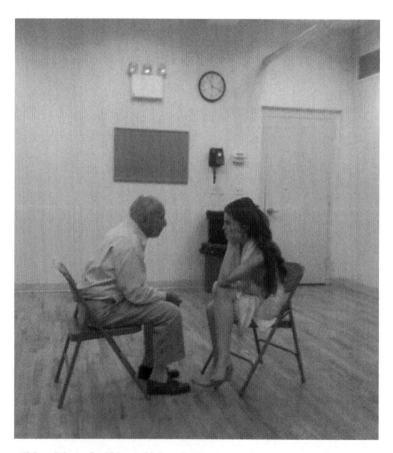

"I Just Met a Girl Named Maria": *The day Josefina Scaglione flew in from Buenos Aires to audition for Maria, Arthur ordered everyone but me (and my trusty iPhone camera) out of the room. Note the eagerness and determination in body language from the twenty-year-old and the ninety-year-old.*

speak English here!" And then variations on "Go fuck yourself." A hundred years ago in the army, I heard a soldier refer to a girl as a "fucking virgin" and realized that a good old English word had lost its good meaning. Today the loss of a good meaning continues with "sucks," as in the denigrating "It sucks."

The difference between this production of *West Side Story* and all others was more than the introduction of Spanish: it was the introduction of acting. That was dangerous to mention because it was causing major problems in Washington. Acting had become as important as dancing and singing. No one in the original or in any of the replicas touring the country and the world had acted or had been directed to act.

In Washington, Matt Cavenaugh as Tony and Cody Green as Riff were weak. The glowing strength of the show was a beautiful twenty-one-year-old gift from Buenos Aires, Josefina Scaglione as Maria (until she was twenty-two). Josa adored Matt, not in any sexual or romantic way, but as a floundering soul she could help. And she did. She and I worked in tandem to make him into Tony. We more or less succeeded through the opening in New York and the Tonys. Then Matt reverted to being the preppy if overage juvenile he was comfortable playing. It was damaging to the production, and his contract wasn't renewed. His understudy, Matthew Hydzik, made the love story the center of the play as it should be, but it was the Maria-Tony story until the last months of the run, when a twenty-four-year-old future star with the memorable name of Matt Shingledecker arrived to make it the Tony-Maria story.

Replacing the adorable little ruffian Jets of the original production with angry, potential killers got the lift it needed when John Arthur Greene took over as Riff. The Jets had a leader; that made every gang member tougher. But they were undercut by adhering to the original choreographed staging of their scenes, which had them constantly punching and feinting and jabbing at one another. "Aren't we tough?" they were saying. No, they weren't; they were cute. If the toughness, the hostility, the anger had been internalized, it would come searing across the footlights. It was and it did.

I used *The Sopranos* to illustrate my point. Those Jersey gangsters rarely punched, but when one did, the punch was like ringing a doorbell. The poor sucker who opened the door was whacked with gunshots. Punching wasn't kidding in Jersey, it was prelude to murder.

Standing still and staring can be very frightening to behold. It's not easy to do; the actor has to believe that what he is feeling is coming across to the audience. Musical performers are so unused to this that it's very hard for most of them. But the dancers in *West Side* became actors. One carried Uta Hagen's book on acting in his backpack and used it.

The satisfaction that brings is immeasurable.

Out of town with a big musical, there isn't time for a haircut, let alone for walking pneumonia, which I had but didn't know it. I felt fluish so I got the Z pack; that always did the trick. An obsessive/compulsive doesn't recognize exhaustion.

Opening night in New York was a blur. People, camera; a smile fixed in place like a denture. Waiting for me when I arrived at the huge opening night party somewhere in space was John Barlow, the show's press agent but my good friend. John knew I was a candidate for the hospital. He also knew hospitals are easy to get into but hard to get out of alive. No surprise that Sloan-Kettering comes to my relentless mind. Well, Tom is there, always, sitting on the edge of the bed in his blue hospital gown.

A Boy Like That: *Arthur in an unusual location on Maria's bed in a rehearsal for* West Side Story. *The sign outside the window says it all.*

John shepherded me through the people and cameras and tables. Even in my blur, I was grateful.

After blurring out *West Side Story's* opening night, I picked myself up and transferred to the George Street Playhouse across the river in New Brunswick for a new play of mine, *New Year's Eve.* I was so glad to be back there that I felt better—mind over ignored matter. As rehearsals progressed, I went out into orbit again, barely managing to continue as the helpful, approving author all the way to opening night. That accomplished, I gave myself permission to collapse.

The collapse was aided by an almost lethal mixture of anti-flu drugs and sleeping pills taken from a deep drawer in the filing cabinet of a too-generous, hypochondriacal friend. How magically they didn't work. I lay in bed unable to sleep for two long days and never-ending nights. My hands shook so I couldn't feed myself; my legs wouldn't allow me to walk, my eyes to read. I opted to check out. Tom was gone; the void was an all-swallowing octopus; just go.

People who say "Have the pills ready for me when . . ." don't take them. I waited until a moderately reasonable seven o'clock the second morning, showered and dressed—easy for a compulsive—and called the doctor. Death, apparently, was not an option. The doctor chided me for waiting to call and would have made a house call (he had twice before), but I was into my invincible act: I would get a car to take me to his hospital, Mt. Sinai.

Michael Marin, his name is; one of the heads of Mt. Sinai. Two years earlier, I'd been told I needed a carotid artery operation. By then, I had learned if cutting is the option, get a second opinion. Michael Marin is the leading surgeon in the country for that operation. I got to him through a rich friend. The meaning of "rich" today is not what it was in the sixties. A friend walking along the beach in Quogue back then told me he had a million dollars and I thought, wow, he's rich. I don't think we said "wow" back then, but no matter. The friend who got me to Marin had a million dollars for pocket money. That's rich.

"I love performing that operation," Marin told me. "I would love to perform it on you. But you don't need it."

He also loved *Gypsy*.

Unlike the usual *Gypsy* aficionado, he had two grown children—he didn't look it—was divorced but had a girlfriend—he did look it—who was also a surgeon—she didn't look it. He appointed himself my internist.

Marin claims that by the time I called him, the pneumonia was waning because of sheer determination on my part. Maybe. I wanted a pill from him that would knock me out, rid me of feeling I was the walking dead, finish me off, bring me back to life, to anyplace except where I was. He called in his pal, a head Mt. Sinai cardiologist whom he had sent me to before. They examined me inside out while they made jokes and I made jokes back—even death at the door couldn't stop my jokes—until they sent me home with a prescription for sleeping pills I was not to take until eight o'clock that night.

That made for the most difficult day I've ever sat through. I literally sat, watching the clock, nothing else. I couldn't eat, couldn't drink, couldn't read, couldn't anything but sit and watch the clock. Tom's brother came by. He'd been on a trip somewhere and told me all about it. I didn't hear, just kept looking at my watch. I didn't make it to eight o'clock. At seven-thirty, I took a sleeping pill and slept for thirteen hours. The next evening, another pill, another thirteen hours. I awoke stronger than ever, full of piss and vinegar, and bounced off to see how *West Side Story* had been doing while Daddy was away.

Just walking into the George Street Playhouse for the meet and greet for *New Year's Eve* made me happy. George Street was home; everyone who worked there was family. They all had driven out to Quogue—a journey from Jersey—for the surprise party Alan Best and David Saint had thrown for Tom and me to celebrate our fiftieth anniversary. Tom had connected with every one of them; his death was a personal loss for everyone at George Street.

Opening night was a smashing success. The laughs were huge, the applause was loud, God was in heaven and all was right with the George Street world. Nonetheless, it was during the run of *New Year's Eve* that I went through that self-inflicted hell and finally recovered in time to be clearheaded and -eyed at the final performance.

The day after *New Year's Eve* ended its run at George Street, the fat lady had sung; it was time to move on. The pleasure, especially when I direct, is in bringing the play to life. It's a short life in regional theatre, but if the theatre is the George Street Playhouse, it's a life well worth it.

It's different for the actors. Rehearsal time is limited. By opening night, they have a good grasp of the character, the shape is clear; now they are ready to fill in details, the nuances, to make the role completely theirs. Closing night is bittersweet. They accept well-earned praise at the party as they nurse a drink or toss down a few; they've thrived on the pleasure of practicing their profession—and it is a profession; it demands skill and craft, which aren't as plentiful as they used to be. In any medium. Another "Oh, you should have been there in the Golden Age" lament? Perhaps, but that doesn't make it any less valid.

Actors understandably think and hope the play they have worked so hard on will transfer to New York. That did happen in the

Young at Heart: *Arthur became downright flirtatious with Marlo Thomas
(here with Natasha Gregson Wagner and Keith Carradine) during
rehearsals of* New Year's Eve. *He thought Marlo was
a "helluva talent" and exclaimed before opening,
"Marlo, where have you been all my life?"*

Golden Age; not these days, though. Today if a show is going to be transferred from George Street to New York—or from most any regional theatre, I would think—the producer doing the transferring is already in place. As is a star; rarely does a production move without one. Reluctant stars will be the death of the new play in New York.

The summer after *New Year's Eve* ended the George Street Playhouse season was the first time since Tom died that I was happy in his house. It was his house, always. The last years, each of us had his own house in Quogue. Having your own space benefits a long-term relationship; at St. Luke's Place, Tom had his office, I had my study.

There can also be space in the same room. When we skied St. Moritz, Tom would meditate every morning, sitting on the far side of the bed, bent over a small AA meditation book, his back to the room. I did floor exercises on the other side of the bed, hidden from him because I was below the bed and his line of vision. No grunting as I went through my same old routine, so he couldn't hear me, either. I gave him space. Of course, space takes money; thankfully, we had enough. You don't have to be rich to forget how money improves life.

The beach house is home to me. It no longer has a guest room; that's become the television room, used mainly to watch tennis. I've never lived here with anyone other than Tom, so in a way he's still here, with Leona, our giant schnauzer, faithfully by his side. Their photograph is at my bedside. In spite of the amount of glass in the bedroom, as in all the rooms, and the plethora of sunlight, it hasn't faded any more than I have. But it has faded.

This house of views of water, ocean and bay, will always be home. Sometimes, especially when this book has been going well, I seem to be aging backwards and getting stronger. Then the writing gets hard and my feet and hands wobble. So it's status quo again. Common sense says it can't go on too much longer this way, but if it doesn't, I still won't move out of the beach house. Tom added a whole wing to his house for me; I've stayed there; I also stayed there before the new wing. But I work at the beach house; I sleep here, I eat breakfast here; everything else at his house. It's called Tom's house by everyone, not only those who knew him well. Just as Tom's park will always be Tom's park. That's being remembered with love.

Tom wasn't perfect. Well, finally! Some will have that reaction. His Achilles heel was his family.

He bought and renovated a house that had been a stable in the Golden Crescent section of Quogue and turned it into a charming, idiosyncratic home for his parents and his younger brother, David. He wanted the love of his family and never gave up on trying to get it. In vain. Is it always in vain with families? With love, "You either got it, or you ain't." From *Gypsy*, if memory serves.

Oscar Hatcher, Tom's father, was a geologist, born in Indian Territory that became part of the state of Oklahoma. He was a kick in the ass. When the Seventh-day Adventists came a-proselytizing, Oscar wouldn't let them leave until he had delivered a history lesson refuting their claims one by one. His son Tom, when the Presbyterian minister came a-collecting, told the minister he was gay and to stop wasting his time and Tom's.

Enola, Tom's mother, had been a librarian; she took over the Quogue library for a time. She was happy in Quogue with its bridge parties and lunches and thin tomato-and-cucumber tea sandwiches and church socials. Enola was in her element and popular.

She once called me to ask why Tom thought she didn't love him.

"Because you don't, and he knows it."

"Oh," she said. That was all.

He never stopped trying. Some years later, when her mind had started to slip away, the three of us were in his car, driving where I don't remember, but I can see the road we were on in Quiogue. His mother was sitting in front next to him. They had been singing when she stopped abruptly to announce:

"I think I'd like to die."

"I'll die with you," Tom said.

She thought about that. Then she turned to him. "You'd do that for me?"

"Oh, yes."

She looked at him, thought about his thinking she didn't love him, and decided she did love him. Not because she was his mother, but because he was Tom. I don't know that she thought all that, but she should have. And if she didn't, perhaps it was because Tom resembled his father and his brother resembled her.

"Well," she said, "then I won't die."

"Then I won't, either," Tom said.

They both laughed and resumed singing.

His brother, David Hatcher, was seven years younger and a talented architect. He designed the two houses on the edge of Tom's park: one that Tom lived in, the other that Alan and Shelley Best live in. There was to be a third, but David never got around to it. Tom waited and nudged and hoped, but real estate is a business. He finally gave up and got another architect. Symbolic of what was right and wrong with them as brothers.

Seven years younger, David was always in the shadow of a terrific-looking brother who didn't know or care that he was terrific-looking, a brother seemingly everybody wanted to like them, a brother who led a seemingly glamorous life and who—sin of sins—wanted the best for his younger brother. Resentment one day; love the next.

But Tom was inconsistent. He wanted David to be independent but also to need him. The last year of his life, he had David move in with him. Years before, the guest room at St. Luke's Place had become permanently David's room.

The arrangement was fine with me. Tom worried constantly about David; I wanted Tom to stop worrying. When Tom died, he left David several million dollars. More than enough to enable him to retire and be independent and have the life of his own Tom always wanted for him.

And that's how it has turned out. He's a new David—alive, fun, laughing, looking at the bright side, but neither blind to the dark nor ducking it. He's happier; he looks better; he even dresses like a new man—colors and more pizzazz. We talk regularly and lunch often. Next week, he's going to tell me about his recent trip to India with a group from the old country—Oklahoma.

Invaluable is the word for Marcia Hefter, our photogenic lawyer over in Riverhead. A valuable thing learned from Marcia I pass along; it came in very handy in a situation that had nothing whatsoever to do with law.

It was learned when Tom had a squatter in one of his rent houses and we went to Marcia for help. Her firm, misogynistic like all white-shoe firms, dictated that real estate problems were handled only by those with actual balls. The self-important macho idiot the firm stuck us with not only didn't get the squatter out but came perilously close to losing the house for us. We threatened to leave the firm.

Marcia took over. She looked like a television commercial for Mercedes or L'Oreal when she drove up to the house taken over by the squatter. She wasn't inside very long. When she came out, she was as elegant and unruffled as she when she went in.

"Stay away from him," she said. "He'll be out in twenty minutes." He was.

How did she do it? What did she say to him? What was her secret? That's what I'm passing along.

"It's the difference between men and women," Marcia said with an impish smile, but she was far from kidding. "Men want to win; women want to accomplish the task." That aphorism came in very handy at an unexpected time: a confrontation over "Krupke" with a creator and the estate of a creator during the previews of *West Side Story* in New York.

Insulted is one thing; I was shit on. It was ugly and the shitters got uglier. Patrick Vaccariello, the best music conductor any director could ask for, sat beside me, offended and aghast. One of the producers sat opposite, waiting for it all to be over. I said nothing, wholly concentrated on accomplishing the task. I listened, I let them vent, shit on me some more, and waited. I heard what they wanted, I knew what I was willing to give them, but I also knew what I wanted. When they wound down and gave, they would get. They did, and then so did I. Thanks to Marcia Hefter.

A house reflects its owner's taste, his personality, how he lives. When there is tension, only taste is reflected. My housekeeper Joann and David Hatcher didn't get on. That's like describing Auschwitz as a segregated spa. It wasn't until David left that the house was once again Tom's: a happy house without tension.

In June of that summer, it was a welcoming house to Millie, who came with Simon and Keith to help celebrate their twentieth anniversary. Their twentieth, and they're each only forty-six. They'll have infinitely more years than the fifty-two I boast of having had with Tom. I don't envy them; I regard it as further proof how special they are.

Joann always loved Millie; now she went mad for Simon and Keith. The anniversary dinner for them plus Millie and me and the Bests should have been photographed: the table was that beautiful, the food was more so. The English sure can sock away the booze and wine and not show it except by being more joyous—if that was humanly possible.

We all laughed as we hadn't since Tom was there, in his chair at the head of the table. We were all sitting where we wanted; we were all feeling free to do what we wanted; we were friends who made each other rejoice. It was more than Simon and Keith's anniversary, it was happiness at being home.

In the fall, George Street started its season with *Come Back, Come Back, Wherever You Are,* a play about loss that I'd written and was directing. I thought it would allow me to vent, to ease pain, to temper emotion, to cope better, to live easier without Tom. It didn't; it did nothing. It was a play; the characters were characters; reality was their reality, not mine. *Writing this book, which is my historical fact, does help. I see where I was then, where I am now. Where I'll be tomorrow, I'll find out tomorrow.*

George Street was unusually excited about the upcoming production of *Come Back, Come Back.* They knew it was about Tom and they wanted him to come back. But they also knew who was to be in the cast. Stars, real stars at George Street: Bernadette Peters and Lauren Bacall in person! SRO, except that George Street doesn't have standing room.

Last Cast: *Arthur directing the last cast of his career (*Come Back, Come Back, Wherever You Are*). Jim Bracchitta, Alison Fraser, and Shirley Knight (far left) were treasured collaborators and soul mates. (Others pictured: John Carter, Leslie Lyles, Christopher Howatt and Danny Stone.)*

I wrote the parts specifically for them, which both knew. Neither of them did the play.

Bernadette felt the subject matter was too close to home; she bowed out. Because Bernadette sang, the character sang. So did Alison Fraser, a highlight of the last *Gypsy* I directed, the best Tessie Tura of them all. Alison had lost her husband as Bernadette had; Alison felt the loss as keenly, maybe more so because she wasn't able to perform for over a year; but Alison used the loss for her performance.

What happened with Bacall was like Bacall: straightforward. "Bacall" is how anyone in her orbit refers to her; "Betty" is what her friends call her. Calling her "Lauren" would be like calling Garbo

"Greta." "Baby," as in "Bogie's Baby," is what she was in Hollywood when I first met her. After Bogie died, she came to New York and the stage determined to be known as herself, an actress, nobody's baby. She is now the legendary Lauren Bacall.

Opening night of *West Side Story*, she came up the aisle with a cane. She'd been having knee trouble on and off for too long. About *Come Back, Come Back,* she snapped, "Don't count on me to walk much." That's her style, her way of saying, "I have a problem. I won't be able to walk too much." She barks, but there's no bite, and she's very funny; she always has been. In the Hollywood days, there was a dinner dance for the Shah of Iran. If you can imagine that today. The Shah asked Bogie's Baby if he could have this dance; she answered, "You bet your ass, Shah." Vintage Bacall and she couldn't have been more than twenty-one.

One of her agents called George Street to ask if there were stairs. That's when I knew the play would be done without stars. Bacall doesn't play games. She wasn't happy about why she couldn't do the play, and she felt badly she was letting me down, but those were the facts of her life. We're better friends than ever. A little demonstration of caring can do that.

So—no Lauren Bacall to join no Bernadette Peters; no stars even before production began. In New York, on Broadway, the show would not have gone on. In New Brunswick, at George Street, the show had to go on. That's the disadvantage inherent to Broadway and the advantage in regional theatre for the play and the actors. The box office folk live with it and have fingers crossed: there's always a chance, slim, but a chance, that if the play is good enough and done well enough, the audience will come close to filling the seats. Not on Tuesdays or Wednesdays, though.

There was a curious benefit from the disappearance of the stars that emerged at the first reading of the play for an audience of the usual George Street suspects. To everyone's total surprise, the play they were listening to wasn't the play they had read. It wasn't the play I thought I had written, either. It was better. How so? What had happened?

What the George Streeters had heard as they read the play, what I had heard as I wrote it, wasn't the voice of the wife; it was the voice of Bernadette Peters. It wasn't the voice of the mother-in-law we heard; it was the voice of Lauren Bacall. At the reading, we were hearing the wife. The mother was Shirley Knight, one of the greatest actresses I have ever worked with. Merely directing *Gypsy*, I've worked with enough actresses called great to know who is really a great actress and who is just called one. Shirley Knight is a great actress.

She raised the bar for the other actors like Jim Brachitta. Jim and I have a history. It began in 1989: he was the smart aleck backstage in the burlesque house in *Gypsy;* since then, he's been in I don't know how many of my plays, but he grew and grew; in *Come Back, Come Back,* he played the leading male role: a man willing to settle for what love he could get from a woman limited by loss. He held his own with both Alison and Shirley. I felt as proud as a father.

I was up during rehearsals. While probing deeper and deeper into their characters each day, the cast was helping me discover the play I had written. I was discovering what I had written through the actors I was directing. That was a first. Those rehearsals were undiluted happiness. In the theatre!

Let the good times roll, they used to sing in New Orleans. Not anymore; the singers were black music makers. The theatre good

Here's Laughing with You, Kid": *Old friends Lauren "Betty" Bacall and Arthur.*

times continued to roll for me when I went back to the Palace Theatre and *West Side Story*. It's curious. Those good times didn't lift me emotionally; they should have, but they didn't. Tom? He's always there; this was something more—the hopelessness permeating the country.

But life is all we have; it's not just Column A and Column B, success or money, that's not what it's all about. It's all about love and when you have your equivalent of Tom to love—yes, he was extraordinary, but it's *your* equivalent—when you have that, you have it all. Am I repeating myself? Well, it's worth repeating.

Back at the Palace with Matt Shingledecker, a hunk with eyes that magnetized the audience—standing at the back, women and men could be heard murmuring, "Did you see those eyes?"—and his Maria, Sarah Amengual. Sarah was a charismatic fireball, the smartest girl in the greasepaint world, not daunted by replacing the irreplaceable Josefina, who by then wasn't so irreplaceable, though the company swooned as always. They weren't very supportive during Sarah's final rehearsal—too busy crying for Josefina, who was from Argentina—but when Sarah went on that night, she entered like a star, the audience applauded the star, and the company gave the best performance they had in months.

Sarah was twenty-one; Matt Shingledecker was twenty-four. John Arthur Greene was twenty-one when he replaced a Riff who was crowding thirty; Matt Cavenaugh was over thirty when he began. At the time of the first auditions, that was the average age of the candidates. Two years later, at auditions for replacements and the touring company, the average age was twenty-three. Why? What had happened in two years? The whole country was getting angrier and more hopeless, but the young were opting out. Too bad, because a younger *West Side Story* made a much better *West Side Story*. Maybe kids relate to the material, maybe they're hungrier, less jaded, more innocent, whatever; the show is more alive, more exciting, more immediate.

The audiences laugh more, applaud more, stand more. They're younger, too. The young discover, the old compare.

The very young touring company was a smash in Detroit—I don't recommend Detroit—where it began and somehow sold out. The production was first rate. David Saint had done a terrific job directing it and it featured, among other things, probably the best Riff and Bernardo I had ever seen, Joseph J. Simeone and German Santiago.

Detroit and its suburbs have very few Hispanics, so the Spanish in the show didn't even mean what it did in New York. But the tour will be playing cities where immigration is a big issue. The reaction will vary from booking to booking. Some theatres want the show more because of the Spanish, some wish they weren't stuck with it. For the company? Hold on to your performance is always the answer. It's booked now for almost two years. Financial historic fact.

The City Center's Encores production of *Anyone Can Whistle* bewildered me. It was a campy mess, but the audience loved it extravagantly, laughing like fools. What opinion had hammered to death in 1964 as outrageous, offensive, even annoying, opinion in 2010 hailed as hilarious, ahead of its time, just what Broadway could use to offset the vogue for simplistic rock musicals.

What stood out for me was that an important plot point revolved around bottling water and selling it, and this was at a time when anyone rarely even drank it. Whatever else *Anyone Can Whistle* was or wasn't, it was prescient.

Last Monday, Barbra Streisand came to St. Luke's Place to talk about playing Rose in a new movie of *Gypsy*. She was five minutes early! I was still getting dressed (for her), but Joann took charge and served a splendid tea. Barbra's had some work done, just the right amount; she looked great. She was amazed at how well I looked and asked Joann what she fed me. She wasn't kidding, she really wanted to know.

I said—tentatively, not wanting to put her off—that we were sort of book-ending our relationship. "No, we are, we are!" she said.

We talked for over two hours and could have gone on longer. Not only about *Gypsy*. We both remembered a telephone call we'd had two years ago that changed so much for each of us.

It was a Sunday morning, I was in the middle of my favorite breakfast: fresh squeezed juice, slightly wet omelet, bagel with cream cheese and coffee. It's almost sick how much I love that breakfast and look forward to it. And right in the middle, she calls, ostensibly to ask my advice: should she do the film version of *Sunset Boulevard*, the musical? Some chat about who's the director; then I ask if I can call her back because I'm in the middle of etc.

When I do call, I start with "Barbra, I've changed." She says: "Since Tom died."

That opened the door. "I don't want to talk to anyone who doesn't say what they mean. You're calling about *Gypsy.*"

"Yes. Do you think I can play Rose?"

"No."

"Too old?"

"No. But you'd play for sympathy."

The end? No, the beginning. She said she knew Rose because her mother was Rose. She went into details. Her mother made Rose look like Mother Teresa. That Barbra survived was a testament to her determination. Had she gotten her mother off her back? She thought so. Last Monday, she said when her mother died she felt nothing. The three-hour conversation left me with affection for Barbra and convinced she could play Rose if she cut her fingernails and didn't direct.

On stage, the objective is to *be in the moment*; off stage, the objective is to *live in the now*. And where am I now? In a good place. Not entirely at peace, but is at peace necessarily a good place? It was good for Tom. When he said "I am at peace," he was in a blue hospital gown sitting on the edge of a hospital bed, knowing cancer was killing him. Peace was in those green eyes I see now even in black-and-white photographs. He wanted me to know that death was all right, he was ready. I wasn't ready for his and I'm not for mine.

There was a moment when I thought I was, but *that has completely changed. I've changed in many ways.*

I no longer get angry about what's going on in the country; a change of dubious value. I should be angry that we live in the United Goldman Sachs of America, courtesy of the White House; I should be angry that the president keeps sending soldiers to Afghanistan, where they will be destroyed physically or mentally or both for a political purpose in a war we can't win: I should be angry at his administration's role in the BP oil disaster; I should be angry, above all, that the hope he gave us, he took away.

But then he brought it back with his speech at the Tucson Memorial for those killed or wounded at the Gabrielle Giffords Democratic street corner rally. The madman who went berserk was able to fire thirty bullets because Congress was in thrall to the gun lobby and the National Rifle Association. Obama didn't mention this, but it was a great speech, a speech that the country needed, a speech that will go down in history. I wish that as president, all Obama had to do was make speeches. What a president he would be! What a country this would be!

What does being angry accomplish? When I was young and very angry at the House Un-American Activities Committee's invasion of Hollywood, we fought and kicked and yelled and got imprisoned. I got off easily: I was blacklisted and went into exile in Paris—better than Elba hands down, and I saw so much and learned so much, and oh, God, the food! When I came back, the country was deathly quiet. But we had fought, lots of us, and *together.* That spirit was subdued but not dead; it boiled to the surface to end the Vietnam War. That, I think, was the last time we were fighting *for* something. From then on, voices trying to be heard were *against*—the Supreme

Court and Bush vs. Gore, 9/11, the invasion of Iraq, etc. *Against* isn't as inspirational and it doesn't get the same results. You always try to phrase a battle positively: we weren't *against* the House Un-American Activities Committee, we were *for* the First Amendment. These times, it's only *against* and too much of that, especially because the fight is lost even before it begins if it does begin, courtesy of fistfuls from the lobbyists and a blatantly right-wing Supreme Court bias. The country is showing signs of waking up, but it's rudderless. It needs a leader. It needs the Obama of the Tucson speech to *do.*

It's curious to me how much the political meant to me and how much less it means now. It's not because of time or Obama; it's because of meeting one person who changed my life. No matter what I do or have done professionally, nothing can equal my fifty-two years with Tom Hatcher, the most extraordinary man I ever met. That was what I wanted and that was what I got: love. For me, that's what life is about.

With Tom gone, the friends I love mean even more. Seeing them and being with them is how and why I live. I went into the park this sunny morning to tell Tom. I didn't; I couldn't; that's over. I sat on our bench and thought about him; I even tried to see him again in his battered straw hat riding his lawn mower. That's over, too. He lives where he will always live—in memory and in his park.

I wanted to tell someone, so I e-mailed David in New Brunswick and Millie in Brighton. I will tell Alan tonight at dinner. Friends, love, life. That's never over.

No?

Where am I now, really? Waiting. There's my work: a new play needing a star as plays do these meager days; a newer play underway that has potential.

There's the pleasure, when I'm living at St. Luke's Place, of walking down to the river and the length of the silvery pier to watch the sun dance on the river. Or, when I'm in Quogue, of walking through Tom's park in and out of the alleys of sunlight. Or sitting on the steps of the beach house and watching the sun sparkle on the ocean that edges the wide, long, clean sand.

There's the pleasure of reading a good book or seeing a good film.

There's the great pleasure of loving friends.

My health is good, all things considered. I look better than I should. I don't lust anymore, and that's not good; to me, that says —"age," "old"— which would be manageable if there were love.

"One Hand, One Heart": *Arthur and Tom glowing in the California sun and in the love that carried them through fifty-two years together. Perhaps they are together like this now . . .*

Love is life. Love is Tom. Tom is gone; there really is no life for me without him. So I'm waiting, waiting for a reason for being here, waiting without expectations but with a glimmer of hope. There's always hope.

EPILOGUE

———

Whoever invented life did a goodish job. We have dreams for ourselves; we call them dreams, acknowledging they won't come true. But we hope they will. And then some of them do.

It's all wrapped up in that word, "hope." At the original end of this story—the end of the last chapter—my future looked bleak. I was wondering why I was still around; all that kept me going was "a glimmer of hope." When we say we have hope, do we really hope? Did I really have that glimmer? Was it tangible, or was it in the dream category? For me, it was dream. Then, with the arrival of a letter, came the reason why it's a better bet to stay alive: surprise can be just around the corner.

The story of this book ended in 2010. The first week in 2011, the letter arrived. I looked at the name of the sender and felt a burst of joy. It brought back one of the most glorious periods of my life with Tom. Continual delirious seriousness with Ashley Feinstein—Ashley because he was born in 1937, the year of *Gone with the Wind* and Ashley Wilkes.

We met when he left working in Jule Styne's office to become my assistant on *Invitation to a March*, the first of my plays I directed on Broadway. Tom was in it. Tom and Ashley became friends, and Tom and Ashley and I became friends then and for wonderful years afterward.

Invitation was brilliant in the opinion of Elliot Norton in Boston, but not in the opinion of whoever was the Times critic in New York. Odd that I don't remember, isn't it? When it was over, Ash was off on his own, producing and directing Off Broadway. He had a rich father who, at that moment, was lavishly indulgent. So was Ash when he was flush: once he bought seven pairs of trousers in London, the same day I left my wallet in a taxi.

All did not go well with Ashley's Off-Broadway ventures, and he was out of the theatre and into the strange world of Faith Popcorn, his on-and-off boss but forever friend. The self-coined name Faith Popcorn hints at but doesn't come close to saying what she does and who she is.

Faith is a unique marketing consultant. She spots trends, starts trends, advises and creates, and makes a fortune at it. She's a demanding, terrifying boss but a loyal friend who loves to spend money. She has spent thousands of dollars on clothes for Ashley and vacations for both of them as she hires and fires him with regularity.

Writing this, I realized Ashley has always had an extreme seesaw relationship with America's soul food: moolah. His father spoiled him with a bank account, then stole his inheritance. He himself has been rich, slipping secretly close to poor and way stations in between. But Ashley is always Ashley; he always lives in style. He may have to use the Laundromat in his apartment house basement, but he buys the books and CDs he wants, goes to a gym, and doesn't go for too long without a martini straight up and a glass or two of Chardonnay. Handsome as he is, he has been without a lover except for one short romance, which I match-made. It was ended by a freakish accident: sweet, handsome, loving Don Clement was moving a fridge, there was water in the kitchen, he was electrocuted. This was not an HBO movie. Melodramatic horror happens in ordinary life, and there is no way of taking it well.

Ashley didn't have another romance, because he had a family: Tom and me. What he brought back into my life beginning with that letter is that family. The three of us were inseparable back when. The Upper East Side, St. Luke's Place, Quogue, London, St. Anton, St. Moritz, Paris, we traveled all of them and back, and then Ashley and Tom were no longer friends and the family, like too many families, became dysfunctional. What happened?

Perception is all. What I perceived back then, what Tom perceived, what Ash perceived—each of us saw it differently and each thought what he saw was the reality. I don't think there is any actual reality. AA changed Tom, his life, my life, all was better and happier and easier than it had ever been—in my perception and Tom's. What was it in Ashley's perception? Again, what happened? Why the split?

Ashley went to AA with Tom a few times, but he didn't want the martinis to disappear. For too long I thought that had caused the rift. It contributed, but there was an important more. Ash had made new friends and Tom was vulnerable.

Social life in New York wasn't easy for him. He was Arthur Laurents's boy friend. The cruelty of the theatre world is like a recurrent bad dream, except that you know you're not going to wake up from this one and it's never going to end. My theatre friends drove us to more or less move our life to Quogue. I only learned from Ash how some had hurt Tom. Some I was aware of: some who had stayed in one of Tom's houses, had been taken care of by him, but had written me the bread-and-butter notes. The caste system is ugly in any form.

It was the beginning of my retreat from the social world. All this is ex post facto and painful.

Tom and Ash became friends first, but soon Tom wondered whether Ash was his friend only because of me. Then Ash got some new friends; he went on holiday with them, Tom felt odd man out. Add drinking and not drinking; add the possessiveness that so often corrodes friendship; add love and being loved, add jealousy, add interpreted proof, and down the rabbit hole he went. Today, a hundred years later, Ash admits it was his fault for not giving Tom the reassurance he knew Tom needed.

You would never have known Tom needed reassurance. He always had humor, he always was generous with himself, he radiated contentment to spare. He never seemed to need. Even when he was dying of cancer. His primary concern was that I not know. Denial came easy to me. But his death was and is very difficult for me. Love and death are not rational.

What I missed so much was my life with Tom and Ashley; what Ashley missed so much was his life with Tom and me. What we brought back for each other was that life with Tom. Our memories coincide; they put us in a time and a place no one else could understand or share. We laugh at things that aren't and can't be funny to anyone else; we use that shorthand anyone with a shared history uses. Each of us is the outlet for some of our unused love for Tom.

And what was in that letter that began all this? Ashley had waited fifty years to see Barbra Streisand play Rose in a movie version of

Gypsy, and now it was about to happen. He wrote to say how happy he was for me and Babs. He always called her Babs. During the years of *I Can Get It for You Wholesale* and *Funny Girl* he was as close to Barbra and Elliott Gould as he was to Tom and me. He still reveres her: he bought her book on design. What clearer proof?

The other day he said she probably doesn't remember him. I'm certain she does because of the Brooklyn girl she still is and the homeless friend he still is. It doesn't really matter to either of them or to me. I thought Barbra and I were bookending our career together, beginning with *Wholesale,* which was her beginning, and ending with *Gypsy,* which would be a fitting finish for her as the movie star she knew from age nineteen she would be. The project ran into an insurmountable obstacle: Warner Brothers refused to give Steve Sondheim and me the approvals we wanted—namely, that our estates have approval after we were gone. I wanted it because the extant record of *Gypsy* is a lousy movie starring a hard-ass, sophisticated Rosalind Russell in black and white pumps lip-synching "Everything's Coming Up Roses." I wanted a new record because theatre is so ephemeral. But, as Steve reminded me, being ephemeral is the essence of theatre. Because a performance, a production, *is* so ephemeral, a different production, a different performance, a different Rose, and another different Rose will keep *Gypsy* alive forever.

A new film version doesn't matter per se. What does matter is that if there is to be one, it be one we can all be proud of. At this moment, it seems very likely it will be an English version. The producer is a jovial Hollywood mogul named Joel Silver—I call him Heigh Ho— who has a Frank Lloyd Wright house in Los Angeles and a Frank Lloyd Wright plantation in South Carolina. He took Barbra to the plantation to spend a few days. Barbra has been famous as a movie star and a recording star for so long that now she is simply famous as Barbra Streisand. Like Elizabeth Taylor. I cannot imagine what it was like for Joel Silver to have Fame Undreamt as a houseguest. After seeing her star footprint in front of his temple and spending time with her listening to her ideas, he asked me to be a producer of the new film of *Gypsy*—not an executive producer, an active functioning producer. He says I am the only one Barbra will listen to.

Perhaps. There are elements in our relationship that are far beyond the professional Barbra—Jim Brolin in her case, Tom Hatcher in mine.

I can see Tom's face the first time I saw him, coming towards me at William B. Riley, the exclusive Beverly Hills men's store he was managing; I can see Tom's face the last time I saw him, sitting on the edge of his hospital bed where he died later that night. I knew then and I know now that this is what life was about, is about. Nothing else; not sitting on the steps of the beach house, looking at the long stretch of sand and the endless ocean; not sitting on our bench in his park and seeing him in my mind's eye riding his mower with his broken straw hat shielding him from the sun; not that closing night of *Gypsy* at City Center with Patti LuPone, the audience applauding and applauding, refusing to leave the theatre. Nothing. The fifty-two years with him, I will always be grateful for, but I will never not miss him. I am now ninety-three and it's all truer than ever.

Ninety-three! Oh, the glory of old age! The splendor! The serenity! Have you ever heard a nonagenarian say that? Have you ever read it? Well, you're not going to read it here. Ninety-three is certifiably old age, and there isn't one physical plus to old age. Everything that was easy before you were firmly in your nineties gets less easy and shows signs that before long it will be difficult.

Permanently difficult. My eye was on reaching 100—why not? I felt that good, and everyone told me how amazingly good I looked— when a shortness of breath sent me to a doctor who diverted it to a discovery that stopped me dead in my tracks. There is more to a doctor than his skill. There is his basic character, the way he regards the specimens of the human race he puts under his microscope. At the up end of the spectrum is my friend, Dr. Michael Marin of Mt. Sinai. "We will beat this thing," he assures me. Midway is Dr. Newsha Godshi: Persian charm, a compassionate heart, a sense of humor (rare in the world of stethoscopes), and an incisive intelligence that gained her my confidence. And last, the eminent Park Avenue pulmonary specialist who, it was evident early, got off on disaster. He thrived on it, he sought it, he practically smacked his lips when he informed me I had a cancerous tumor on my lungs. His joy and enthusiasm increased exponentially as he whipped out the ace up his sleeve: "Probably malignant."

Did he frighten me? Yes. All my whining about "Why am I still here?" was balls. I wanted desperately to stay here, to make plans with loving friends, to breathe the air through the car window as I travel, even if it's to or from another test from another specialist. Today, stress—four hours; tomorrow, a PET/CT scan. An MRI. Tuesday, a bronchoscopy, when a biopsy will be taken and determine what I have and how it can be dealt with. Radiation, not surgery. At ninety-three, radical surgery can result in a quality of life not worth living. Is the quality of life I'm living now so hot? It's living crippled by illness. Is that living? Isn't it existing?

For the first time in more than fifty years, I don't do my floor exercises. Because I can't. I no longer take my regular walks down to the river and out along the handsome new pier. Because I can't. Malignant or benign, the tumor will have to be dealt with.

And when it is pinpointed and treatment planned, then what? There are more variables than I thought; cancer is more treatable than it used to be; it's no longer a sure death sentence. But contemplating my future, what do I see? Tuesday. That procedure on Tuesday. I will have to undergo an anesthetic. I believe I won't come out from under. "Believe" is really "hope"; wishful thinking. This is the best answer for me.

There is no pleasure in existing, in being constantly tired, constantly aware of a dull pain in the right shoulder, constantly afraid to cough or do something that will start coughing. In making it through the days and the nights—oh, the nights! I don't know which are worse— in making it through them physically limited, handicapped. Before this, I dreaded a stroke; now, I think this must be worse. But I've never had a stroke. Or a heart attack. Just cancer. Cancer is worse; it must be.

I say nothing about this to anyone, not even David. There's nothing he can do about it; it would only upset him even more. What he can do, he does so expertly, so lovingly that anything I can do not to exacerbate his concern, I must do.

The other evening, when Ashley came by, I said, "Ash, I'm in a very different world from the one I was in the last time you came by." That had been BC: Before Cancer.

I've been in several different worlds, we all have. An early one was the heat-laden night driving with Tom down Santa Monica Canyon the summer we met. "You don't know it, but you're in love with me," he said. That was a new world, but even before I had fully adjusted to it, he took me into yet another world when he came to New York and moved in with me, into my one-bedroom apartment on the Upper East Side, prized for its sunken living room with mirrored fireplace wall. Just the two of us, openly; not three, four pals, guys; no beards for the den: no Playboy Bunnies, pearl and cashmere wearers, actresses, dancers. Two young fellows did not do that in 1955. If they did, they risked being called homosexual. Which is most likely what Tom and I were called. We didn't think about that; it didn't occur to us; we didn't care. Not for fifty-two years, a great many of which were spent in a small village with a lot of churches on the South Shore of Long Island. We didn't hide, we didn't flaunt, but we didn't care. Oddly enough, that seemed to make the churchgoers not care. Not caring was a large reason those years were so splendid.

Perhaps because those years were so splendid, so extraordinary, this year is so appalling. All this focus on Tuesday's procedure. The biopsy and then what? What I would like is for it to lead to the end of just existing. If not that, then I would like it to lead quickly to the end. I never thought I could say that, but I never knew what it was like to feel like this. This world I'm in is not one I want to stay in.

At one of the scans the other day, the very young, bearded technician said to me as I hopped off the slab that had carried me into the machine's tunnel: "I want to be like you when I'm ninety-three." I didn't respond as I wanted to. What for? It might be quite different for him. I hope it will be. In any event, he should be allowed to find out for himself. So I just smiled and said, "Thank you." And wondered then, as now, am I going to have a relatively happy ending?

CODA

———

"Am I going to have a relatively happy ending?"

Those were the last words Arthur wrote.

I now add this coda to let you, the reader know that his ending was just that, "relatively happy."

Arthur was my best friend, and I his. I was also his health care proxy and power of attorney, so I saw him through the ten days that remained of his life following those final words he wrote.

But in true Arthur style, the last scene of his life was filled with dramatic twists and turns.

The bronchoscopy procedure on that following Tuesday did not happen as planned. Instead, he called me on Sunday at rehearsal of a play I was directing and said in very weak, short breaths that he "needed me desperately." I drove in and, the moment I saw him, put him in the car and took him to the ER at Mt. Sinai.

There, a fast x-ray later, they inserted a large tube into his lung and drained almost two liters of fluid: he was drowning in his own lung fluids.

The bronchoscopy was moved up and done first thing Monday.

And then the dramatic twist: his doctor, a young man whom Arthur liked after dissatisfaction with so many others, one he described as a "Paul Reiser from *Mad About You*" named Todd Weiser, came to me from the OR, face ashen, head shaking, and said "It's a miracle! After two hours inside, I can't find one trace of cancer! He could live another ten years!"

Incomprehensible joy!

But when Arthur finally awoke from the anesthesia and I told him the extraordinary news, he looked strangely disappointed. I didn't understand that look until his trusted agent, Jonathan Lomma, sent me the epilogue Arthur had just confidentially e-mailed him: the only segment of his writings that he had not sent me to proof for my reactions in almost twenty years! And I now know why.

For Arthur had written his last. And with nothing left to write, there was nothing left to live.

Physically, the "large mass" on his lung that three separate doctors, even the head of thoracic surgery at a major hospital, had all presumed was a cancerous tumor, was actually an inflammation caused by aspirated food caught in his bronchia and trachea, which had become lodged and caused infectious pneumonia. Arthur was always impatient, even about eating. The large aforementioned tube needed to stay in for days, and caused Arthur considerable pain and discomfort. Recovery would be slow and arduous, including intravenous antibiotics continuously. This was not a life Arthur wanted, one of being an invalid and unable to create. In fact, in ninety-three years, Arthur had never once been in the hospital (just before he went in for the bronchoscopy, doctors came to us and asked, "Is there a mistake on this form? You've never been in the hospital, ever, and never had an operation?" To which Arthur replied:

"Yes, one operation: Circumcision." Laugh. And blackout. But true.

But even more than that, I could see that he wanted to go; he had already written it, as I read later in his epilogue.

He wanted to go home, and, after much arguing with many doctors (it's tougher to get someone out of the hospital than to get him in), I managed to get him back home to his own bed, where he smiled, grabbed me by the arm, and said, "Thank you."

Of course, without the tubes etc. it would probably be only a matter of time. A lovely palliative care doctor talked us through it, giving the private nurse we hired medications that would ease his pain and slow down his breathing. This doctor also talked to us about the different matters we needed to discuss, including goodbyes. The doctor recommended dividing friends into three groups: first, those he wanted to see to say goodbye; second, those good friends he wanted to let know of his condition but didn't have the strength to see; and third, those who would just have to find out later.

Typical of Arthur, he said, "No one," but then relented and asked for six people. Two lived far away; the other four immediately came. Interestingly, none of them were in "The Biz."

And the very next day, on May 5, with a few of us sitting next to him on the bed, he just calmly and quietly, simply stopped breathing.

"Relatively happy."

And I hope in some way with his Tom again.

In the days that followed, hundreds of articles appeared all around the world about this great man of the theatre.

Personally, I was dismayed that so many whom I had seen only be gracious and lovely to Arthur in person, and some of whom had had perhaps their greatest successes professionally with him, decided to dish him in public. Ironic, because those people, like everyone else, knew what Arthur thought of them, because he always told them. They wouldn't have to wait to hear "what he really thought" about them in a newspaper. Perhaps schadenfreude is just a part of human nature, or perhaps newspaper editors, even the *New York Times*, quoting *New York Magazine*'s hatchet job profile of Arthur, continue to believe that only dirt sells.

In any event, there was another Arthur Laurents, different from the one who had been cast in the role of the feared truth-telling legend of Broadway, a role I believe he sometimes enjoyed playing.

That Arthur Laurents was brilliant and funny and so loving. And he was my best friend.

—D<small>AVID</small> S<small>AINT</small>

INDEX

in *Mainly on Directing: "Gypsy,"
"West Side Story," and Other
Musicals*, 157–58
national tour of, 147, 176–77
negative criticism of, 158–59
in *New York Magazine*, 104–7
opening night of, 160, 173
original auditions for, 58
original creators of, 13, 52–53,
133
original inspiration for, 52–
53
production costs for, 158
Santiago as Bernardo in, 176
Santiago in, 176

Shingledecker in, 106, 159,
175–76
Simeone in, 176
success of revival of, 79
Tony Awards for, 106
Washington tryouts for, 157–58
Wolsky, Albert, *110*, 111
World War II
Assignment Home, 23–24
The Knife, 24
New York City during, 28–29, 118
radio propaganda during, 30–31
sexual freedom during, 28–29

Youmans, Jim, 109

Printed in Great Britain
by Amazon

33186520R00126